Sheila S. Intner, DLS, MLS, BA
Sally C. Tseng, MLS, BA
Mary Lynette Larsgaard, MA, BA
Editors

Electronic Cataloging: AACR2 and Metadata for Serials and Monographs

Electronic Cataloging: AACR2 and Metadata for Serials and Monographs has been co-published simultaneously as *Cataloging & Classification Quarterly*, Volume 36, Numbers 3/4 2003.

Pre-publication REVIEWS, COMMENTARIES, EVALUATIONS . . .

"TIMELY. . . . Addresses a rapidly evolving area of critical importance to the library profession. The twelve contributing authors represent SOME OF THE MOST IMPORTANT THINKERS AND PRACTITIONERS IN CATALOGING."

Peggy Johnson, MBA, MA
Associate University Librarian
University of Minnesota Libraries

More pre-publication
REVIEWS, COMMENTARIES, EVALUATIONS . . .

"**I**MPRESSIVE in both its range and vision. . . . WIDE-RANGING AND PERCEPTIVE . . . explores all the highlights–from AACR, ISBD, MARC, and ISSN, to Dublin Core, Description of Works of Art, Object ID, and VRA Core Categories; from encoding schemas to metadata schemas; and from metadata strategy to implementation issues. The book frequently surprised this reader with new views of well-established standards and fresh looks at their roles in electronic cataloging."

Marcia Lei Zeng, PhD
Associate Professor
Kent State University

"**V**ALUABLE . . . COMFORTING AND INSPIRING. The overall aspect of the chapters is forward-looking, with many chapters concentrating on the vision of significant change, while others speak of particular experimental applications of new standards and technologies. Yet the strength of the volume as a whole may lie in the degree to which the discussions of change and unfamiliar concepts is placed firmly in the context of the principles of librarianship and existing standards such as AACR2, and related to how libraries have engineered and handled radical advancement in the past, and how they continue to do so."

Janet Swan Hill, MA
Editor of Education for Cataloging and the Organization of Information: Pitfalls and the Pendulum
Professor and Associate Director for Technical Services
University of Colorado Libraries
Boulder

The Haworth Information Press
An Imprint of The Haworth Press, Inc.

Electronic Cataloging: AACR2 and Metadata for Serials and Monographs

Electronic Cataloging: AACR2 and Metadata for Serials and Monographs has been co-published simultaneously as *Cataloging & Classification Quarterly*, Volume 36, Numbers 3/4 2003.

Cataloging & Classification Quarterly™ Monographic "Separates"

Below is a list of "separates," which in serials librarianship means a special issue simultaneously published as a special journal issue or double-issue *and* as a "separate" hardbound monograph. (This is a format which we also call a "DocuSerial.")

"Separates" are published because specialized libraries or professionals may wish to purchase a specific thematic issue by itself in a format which can be separately cataloged and shelved, as opposed to purchasing the journal on an on-going basis. Faculty members may also more easily consider a "separate" for classroom adoption.

"Separates" are carefully classified separately with the major book jobbers so that the journal tie-in can be noted on new book order slips to avoid duplicate purchasing.

You may wish to visit Haworth's Website at . . .

http://www.HaworthPress.com

. . . to search our online catalog for complete tables of contents of these separates and related publications.

You may also call 1-800-HAWORTH (outside US/Canada: 607-722-5857), or Fax 1-800-895-0582 (outside US/Canada: 607-771-0012), or e-mail at:

docdelivery@haworthpress.com

Electronic Cataloging: AACR2 and Metadata for Serials and Monographs, edited by Sheila S. Intner, DLS, MLS, BA, Sally C. Tseng, MLS, BA, and Mary Lynette Larsgaard, MA, BA (Vol. 36, No. 3/4, 2003). *"The twelve contributing authors represent some of the most important thinkers and practitioners in cataloging." (Peggy Johnson, MBA, MA, Associate University Librarian, University of Minnesota Libraries)*

Historical Aspects of Cataloging and Classification, edited by Martin D. Joachim, MA (classical languages and literatures), MA (library science) (Vol. 35, No. 1/2, 2002 and Vol. 35, No. 3/4, 2003). *Traces the development of cataloging and classification in countries and institutions around the world.*

Education for Cataloging and the Organization of Information: Pitfalls and the Pendulum, edited by Janet Swan Hill, BA, MA (Vol. 34, No. 1/2/3, 2002). *Examines the history, context, present, and future of education for cataloging and bibliographic control.*

Works as Entities for Information Retrieval, edited by Richard P. Smiraglia, PhD (Vol. 33, No. 3/4, 2002). *Examines domain-specific research about works and the problems inherent in their representation for information storage and retrieval.*

The Audiovisual Cataloging Current, edited by Sandra K. Roe, MS (Vol. 31, No. 2/3/4, 2001). *"All the great writers, teachers, and lecturers are here: Olson, Fox, Intner, Weihs, Weitz, and Yee. This eclectic collection is sure to find a permanent place on many catalogers' bookshelves. . . . Something for everyone. . . . Explicit cataloging guidelines and AACR2R interpretations galore." (Verna Urbanski, MA, MLS, Chief Media Cataloger, University of North Florida, Jacksonville)*

Managing Cataloging and the Organization of Information: Philosophies, Practices and Challenges at the Onset of the 21st Century, edited by Ruth C. Carter, PhD, MS, MA (Vol. 30, No. 1/2/3, 2000). *"A fascinating series of practical, forthright accounts of national, academic, and special library cataloging operations in action. . . . Yields an abundance of practical solutions for shared problems, now and for the future. Highly recommended." (Laura Jizba, Head Cataloger, Portland State University Library, Oregon)*

The LCSH Century: One Hundred Years with the Library of Congress Subject Headings System, edited by Alva T. Stone, MLS (Vol. 29, No. 1/2, 2000). *Traces the 100-year history of the Library of Congress Subject Headings, from its beginning with the implementation of a dictionary catalog in 1898 to the present day, exploring the most significant changes in LCSH policies and practices, including a summary of other contributions celebrating the centennial of the world's most popular library subject heading language.*

Maps and Related Cartographic Materials: Cataloging, Classification, and Bibliographic Control, edited by Paige G. Andrew, MLS, and Mary Lynette Larsgaard, MA, BA (Vol. 27, No. 1/2/3/4, 1999). *Discover how to catalog the major formats of cartographic materials, including sheet maps, early and contemporary atlases, remote-sensed images (i.e., aerial photographs and satellite images), globes, geologic sections, digital material, and items on CD-ROM.*

Portraits in Cataloging and Classification: Theorists, Educators, and Practitioners of the Late Twentieth Century, edited by Carolynne Myall, MS, CAS, and Ruth C. Carter, PhD (Vol. 25, No. 2/3/4, 1998). *"This delightful tome introduces us to a side of our profession that we rarely see: the human beings behind the philosophy, rules, and interpretations that have guided our professional lives over the past half century. No collection on cataloging would be complete without a copy of this work." (Walter M. High, PhD, Automation Librarian, North Carolina Supreme Court Library; Assistant Law Librarian for Technical Services, North Carolina University, Chapel Hill)*

Cataloging and Classification: Trends, Transformations, Teaching, and Training, edited by James R. Shearer, MA, ALA, and Alan R. Thomas, MA, FLA (Vol. 24, No. 1/2, 1997). *"Offers a comprehensive retrospective and innovative projection for the future." (The Catholic Library Association)*

Electronic Resources: Selection and Bibliographic Control, edited by Ling-yuh W. (Miko) Pattie, MSLS, and Bonnie Jean Cox, MSLS (Vol. 22, No. 3/4, 1996). *"Recommended for any reader who is searching for a thorough, well-rounded, inclusive compendium on the subject." (The Journal of Academic Librarianship)*

Cataloging and Classification Standards and Rules, edited by John J. Reimer, MLS (Vol. 21, No. 3/4, 1996). *"Includes chapters by a number of experts on many of our best loved library standards. . . . Recommended to those who want to understand the history and development of our library standards and to understand the issues at play in the development of new standards." (LASIE)*

Classification: Options and Opportunities, edited by Alan R. Thomas, MA, FLA (Vol. 19, No. 3/4, 1995). *"There is much new and valuable insight to be found in all the chapters. . . . Timely in refreshing our confidence in the value of well-designed and applied classification in providing the best of service to the end-users." (Catalogue and Index)*

Cataloging Government Publications Online, edited by Carolyn C. Sherayko, MLS (Vol. 18, No. 3/4, 1994). *"Presents a wealth of detailed information in a clear and digestible form, and reveals many of the practicalities involved in getting government publications collections onto online cataloging systems." (The Law Librarian)*

Cooperative Cataloging: Past, Present and Future, edited by Barry B. Baker, MLS (Vol. 17, No. 3/4, 1994). *"The value of this collection lies in its historical perspective and analysis of past and present approaches to shared cataloging. . . . Recommended to library schools and large general collections needing materials on the history of library and information science." (Library Journal)*

Languages of the World: Cataloging Issues and Problems, edited by Martin D. Joachim (Vol. 17, No. 1/2, 1993). *"An excellent introduction to the problems libraries must face when cataloging materials not written in English. . . . should be read by every cataloger having to work with international materials, and it is recommended for all library schools. Nicely indexed." (Academic Library Book Review)*

Retrospective Conversion Now in Paperback: History, Approaches, Considerations, edited by Brian Schottlaender, MLS (Vol. 14, No. 3/4, 1992). *"Fascinating insight into the ways and means of converting and updating manual catalogs to machine-readable format." (Library Association Record)*

Enhancing Access to Information: Designing Catalogs for the 21st Century, edited by David A. Tyckoson (Vol. 13, No. 3/4, 1992). *"Its down-to-earth, nontechnical orientation should appeal to practitioners including administrators and public service librarians." (Library Resources & Technical Services)*

Describing Archival Materials: The Use of the MARC AMC Format, edited by Richard P. Smiraglia, MLS (Vol. 11, No. 3/4, 1991). *"A valuable introduction to the use of the MARC AMC format and the principles of archival cataloging itself." (Library Resources & Technical Services)*

Subject Control in Online Catalogs, edited by Robert P. Holley, PhD, MLS (Vol. 10, No. 1/2, 1990). *"The authors demonstrate the reasons underlying some of the problems and how solutions may be sought. . . . Also included are some fine research studies where the researchers have sought to test the interaction of users with the catalogue, as well as looking at use by library practitioners." (Library Association Record)*

Library of Congress Subject Headings: Philosophy, Practice, and Prospects, by William E. Studwell, MSLS (Supp. #2, 1990). *"Plays an important role in any debate on subject cataloging and succeeds in focusing the reader on the possibilities and problems of using Library of Congress Subject Headings and of subject cataloging in the future." (Australian Academic & Research Libraries)*

Authority Control in the Online Environment: Considerations and Practices, edited by Barbara B. Tillett, PhD (Vol. 9, No. 3, 1989). *"Marks an excellent addition to the field. . . . [It] is intended, as stated in the introduction, to 'offer background and inspiration for future thinking.' In achieving this goal, it has certainly succeeded." (Information Technology & Libraries)*

National and International Bibliographic Databases: Trends and Prospects, edited by Michael Carpenter, PhD, MBA, MLS (Vol. 8, No. 3/4, 1988). *"A fascinating work, containing much of concern both to the general cataloger and to the language or area specialist as well. It is also highly recommended reading for all those interested in bibliographic databases, their development, or their history." (Library Resources & Technical Services)*

Cataloging Sound Recordings: A Manual with Examples, by Deanne Holzberlein, PhD, MLS (Supp. #1, 1988). *"A valuable, easy to read working tool which should be part of the standard equipment of all catalogers who handle sound recordings." (ALR)*

Education and Training for Catalogers and Classifiers, edited by Ruth C. Carter, PhD (Vol. 7, No. 4, 1987). *"Recommended for all students and members of the profession who possess an interest in cataloging." (RQ-Reference and Adult Services Division)*

The United States Newspaper Program: Cataloging Aspects, edited by Ruth C. Carter, PhD (Vol. 6, No. 4, 1986). *"Required reading for all who use newspapers for research (historians and librarians in particular), newspaper cataloguers, administrators of newspaper collections, and–most important–those who control the preservation pursestrings." (Australian Academic & Research Libraries)*

Computer Software Cataloging: Techniques and Examples, edited by Deanne Holzberlein, PhD, MLS (Vol. 6, No. 2, 1986). *"Detailed explanations of each of the essential fields in a cataloging record. Will help any librarian who is grappling with the complicated responsibility of cataloging computer software." (Public Libraries)*

AACR2 and Serials: The American View, edited by Neal L. Edgar (Vol. 3, No. 2/3, 1983). *"This book will help any librarian or serials user concerned with the pitfalls and accomplishments of modern serials cataloging." (American Reference Books Annual)*

The Future of the Union Catalogue: Proceedings of the International Symposium on the Future of the Union Catalogue, edited by C. Donald Cook (Vol. 2, No. 1/2, 1982). *Experts explore the current concepts and future prospects of the union catalogue.*

Electronic Cataloging: AACR2 and Metadata for Serials and Monographs

Sheila S. Intner, DLS, MLS, BA
Sally C. Tseng, MLS, BA
Mary Lynette Larsgaard, MA, BA
Editors

Electronic Cataloging: AACR2 and Metadata for Serials and Monographs has been co-published simultaneously as *Cataloging & Classification Quarterly*, Volume 36, Numbers 3/4 2003.

The Haworth Information Press®
An Imprint of The Haworth Press, Inc.

New York • London • Victoria (AU)
www.HaworthPress.com

Published by

The Haworth Information Press®, 10 Alice Street, Binghamton, NY 13904-1580 USA

The Haworth Information Press® is an imprint of The Haworth Press, Inc., 10 Alice Street, Binghamton, NY 13904-1580 USA.

Electronic Cataloging: AACR2 and Metadata for Serials and Monographs has been co-published simultaneously as *Cataloging & Classification Quarterly*, Volume 36, Numbers 3/4 2003.

The development, preparation, and publication of this work has been undertaken with great care. However, the publisher, employees, editors, and agents of The Haworth Press and all imprints of The Haworth Press, Inc., including The Haworth Medical Press® and Pharmaceutical Products Press®, are not responsible for any errors contained herein or for consequences that may ensue from use of materials or information contained in this work. Opinions expressed by the author(s) are not necessarily those of The Haworth Press, Inc. With regard to case studies, identities and circumstances of individuals discussed herein have been changed to protect confidentiality. Any resemblance to actual persons, living or dead, is entirely coincidental.

Cover design by Jennifer M. Gaska.

Library of Congress Cataloging-in-Publication Data

Electronic cataloging : AACR2 and metadata for serials and monographs / Sheila S. Intner, Sally C. Tseng, Mary Lynette Larsgaard, editors.
    p. cm.
    Papers originally presented at the 2001-2002 Association for Library Collections & Technical Services regional institutes on AACR2 and metadata.
    "Co-published simultaneously as Cataloging & classification quarterly, v. 36, nos. 3/4, 2003."
    Includes bibliographical references and index.
    ISBN 0-7890-2224-9 (alk. paper) – ISBN 0-7890-2225-7 (pbk. : alk. paper)
    1. Cataloging of computer network resources–Congresses. 2. Metadata–Congresses. I. Intner, Sheila S. II. Tseng, Sally C. III. Larsgaard, Mary Lynette, 1946- IV. Cataloging & classification quarterly.
Z695.24.E43 2003
                                      2003009619

Indexing, Abstracting & Website/Internet Coverage

This section provides you with a list of major indexing & abstracting services. That is to say, each service began covering this periodical during the year noted in the right column. Most Websites which are listed below have indicated that they will either post, disseminate, compile, archive, cite or alert their own Website users with research-based content from this work. (This list is as current as the copyright date of this publication.)

(continued)

  *Exact start date to come.

Special Bibliographic Notes related to special journal issues (separates) and indexing/abstracting:

- indexing/abstracting services in this list will also cover material in any "separate" that is co-published simultaneously with Haworth's special thematic journal issue or DocuSerial. Indexing/abstracting usually covers material at the article/chapter level.
- monographic co-editions are intended for either non-subscribers or libraries which intend to purchase a second copy for their circulating collections.
- monographic co-editions are reported to all jobbers/wholesalers/approval plans. The source journal is listed as the "series" to assist the prevention of duplicate purchasing in the same manner utilized for books-in-series.
- to facilitate user/access services all indexing/abstracting services are encouraged to utilize the co-indexing entry note indicated at the bottom of the first page of each article/chapter/contribution.
- this is intended to assist a library user of any reference tool (whether print, electronic, online, or CD-ROM) to locate the monographic version if the library has purchased this version but not a subscription to the source journal.
- individual articles/chapters in any Haworth publication are also available through the Haworth Document Delivery Service (HDDS).

Electronic Cataloging: AACR2 and Metadata for Serials and Monographs

Electronic Cataloging: AACR2 and Metadata for Serials and Monographs has been co-published simultaneously as *Cataloging & Classification Quarterly*, Volume 36, Numbers 3/4 2003.

Electronic Cataloging:
AACR2 and Metadata
for Serials and Monographs

CONTENTS

PART 3. AACR2 AND METADATA

ABOUT THE EDITORS

Sheila S. Intner, DLS, MLS, BA, is a Professor in the Graduate School of Library & Information Science at Simmons College and Founding Director of GSLIS at Mount Holyoke College. Dr. Intner teaches and conducts research in the areas of cataloging and collection development, and also teaches professional writing, bibliographic instruction, and basic materials repair. Winner of the 1989 OnLine Audiovisual Catalogers Award, the 1992 Brubaker Award, and the 1997 Margaret Mann Award for outstanding contribution to cataloging and classification, she has published 16 books, including *Standard Cataloging for School & Public Libraries,* now in its third edition, as well as numerous articles and chapters in books. She edits the monographic series *Frontiers of Access to Library Materials* for ALA Editions and writes the bimonthly "Dollars and Sense" column for *Technicalities.* Recently, she published a study on the impact of the Internet on collection development, and she gave papers in Japan, China, Dallas, and San Diego. Dr. Intner has been elected Chair of OnLine Audiovisual Catalogers, Chair of the Cataloging & Classification Section of the Resources & Technical Services Division of the ALA, President of the Association for Library Collections & Technical Services, and an American Library Association Councilor. She spent a year in Israel as a Senior Fulbright Professor. Dr. Intner was recently named a 2003 Fulbright Senior Specialist.

Sally C. Tseng, MLS, BA, is Executive Director of the Chinese American Librarians Association (CALA). She was Head of Serials Cataloging at the University of Nebraska-Lincoln Libraries from 1968 to 1981, as well as Head of Serials Cataloging and Librarian with Distinguished Rank at the University of California, Irvine (UCI) Libraries from 1981 to 2002. Ms. Tseng is a sought-after speaker, trainer, author, compiler, and editor of numerous books, papers and articles. Her topics include AACR2, automation, cataloging, bibliographic organization, CD-ROMs, digital, electronic and Web resources, metadata, serials standards, and applications of advanced technologies. Ms. Tseng is very active in professional organizations and has made significant contributions to the library community. She has received numerous awards including the CALA Distinguished Service Award, University of California research grants, and the first ALCTS President's Award for contributions to the library and information profession.

Mary Lynette Larsgaard, MA, BA, is Assistant Head of the Map and Imagery Laboratory of the Davidson Library at the University of California in Santa Barbara. The Map and Imagery Lab at UCSB has a collection of remote-sensing imagery and maps of approximately 4.5 million items, and is the largest of its kind in any university library in North America. Ms. Larsgaard is the author of numerous journal articles and several books, including *Maps and Related Cartographic Materials: Cataloging, Classification, and Bibliographic Control* (The Haworth Press, Inc.) and three editions of *Map Librarianship: An Introduction* (Libraries Unlimited). Her specialties include cataloging/metadata creation and twentieth century and more recent topographic and geologic maps. She remains very active in the Map and Geography Round Table of the American Library Association (ALA), the Western Association of Map Libraries and the Anglo-American Cataloguing Committee for Cartographic Materials. She co-chaired, with Sally C. Tseng, the Steering Committee for the ALCTS Preconference on Metadata for the Web and Regional Institutes on AACR2 and Metadata. In the year 2000, she was promoted to Librarian, Step V–a step given only to a librarian who has demonstrated superior competence and is internationally recognized as an authority in library science.

Introduction

Sheila S. Intner
Sally C. Tseng
Mary Lynette Larsgaard

There used to be a time-honored process for publishing the proceedings of scholarly conferences, seminars, and institutes. It was almost automatic, since scholars recognized that the papers delivered in person at the event often were the first opportunities for the results of important research efforts to be revealed, and because the wheels of monographic book publishing turned very slowly. Those results might not reach their desks for years without the publication of the events' proceedings. No matter how large the conference audience might be, many more interested parties either could not make it to the event in person or, if they attended, might not be able to hear all of the papers. Without some kind of publication in hand, they could not follow up their first impressions with second or third re-readings and leisurely reflection. Thus, the published proceedings were able to satisfy the needs of colleagues who were unable to attend a seminar or institute, those who attended but did not hear all of the papers, and those who heard the papers but wished to review and mull over their contents.

Today, times have changed. The automatic publication of proceedings of important scholarly events is no longer automatic. For one thing, the plethora of conferences in any one field makes it difficult for publishers to keep up with the flow of material, particularly if the material is

[Haworth co-indexing entry note]: "Introduction." Intner, Sheila S., Sally C. Tseng, and Mary Lynette Larsgaard. Co-published simultaneously in *Cataloging & Classification Quarterly* (The Haworth Information Press, an imprint of The Haworth Press, Inc.) Vol. 36, No. 3/4, 2003, pp. 1-4; and: *Electronic Cataloging: AACR2 and Metadata for Serials and Monographs* (ed: Sheila S. Intner, Sally C. Tseng, and Mary Lynette Larsgaard) The Haworth Information Press, an imprint of The Haworth Press, Inc., 2003, pp. 1-4. Single or multiple copies of this article are available for a fee from The Haworth Document Delivery Service [1-800-HAWORTH, 9:00 a.m. - 5:00 p.m. (EST). E-mail address: docdelivery@haworthpress.com].

http://www.haworthpress.com/store/product.asp?sku=J104
10.1300/J104v36n03_01

1

likely to be of interest to small circles of readers. The smaller the circle of readers, the less likely the costs of issuing a publication can be recouped. The possibility of failing to cover costs and make something toward profits simply is not good business. For another thing, readers are already being bombarded with ever-larger numbers of materials in their subject areas, causing the more dedicated of them no end of grief over the lack of time to read it all. Thus, readers hesitate to demand more publications from publishers.

Given this state of affairs, we editors were both gratified and grateful when *Cataloging & Classification Quarterly* editor Ruth Carter asked us to prepare this record of the papers delivered at the 2001-2002 Association for Library Collections & Technical Services Regional Institutes on the Anglo-American Cataloguing Rules, 2nd Edition, 2002 Revision and Metadata–its proceedings. It was evidence of the intensity of the interest in the subject as well as the dedication of Haworth Press to bringing important scholarly material to readers.

We approached our task with no small amount of trepidation, in part, because we knew other publications had covered earlier presentations by some of the same experts and we did not wish to duplicate their work; and, in part, because some of the speakers worked solely from notes and outlines, not from full scripts of their presentations. Each of these matters was addressed in turn, and we hope readers of this publication will find the solutions satisfactory.

Regarding the problem of overlap with earlier publications, most notably with Scarecrow Press's excellent monograph, *Cataloging the Web*, a proceedings based on the ALCTS Preconference on Metadata and AACR2 held in Chicago in July, 2000, and ably edited by Wayne Jones, Judith Ahronheim, and Josephine Crawford, we were aided in finding a solution in two ways. First, the roster of speakers at the ALCTS preconference and subsequent regional institutes was not identical, although several individuals were invited to make presentations at both, and did so. Second, the speakers at the 2000 preconference were given somewhere between fifteen and twenty minutes in which to give their remarks, while speakers at the 2001-2002 regional institutes were asked to provide in-depth information for ninety-minute slots. Not only did the conscientious speakers among the institute faculty endeavor to update their presentations by including new material as soon as it became available, but even those speakers who covered topical areas that had experienced little change in the time between the events found themselves having to make extensive additions to their papers to satisfy the new schedule.

Six speakers whose papers were among those included in *Cataloging the Web* are also represented here by greatly revised offerings. They are Murtha Baca, Michael Gorman, Jean Hirons, Sheila S. Intner, Regina Romano Reynolds, and Brian E. C. Schottlaender. Six speakers and their papers are entirely new to this volume. They are Grace Agnew, Ann Huthwaite, Erik Jul, Yuan-liang Ma, Wei Liu, and Barbara B. Tillett. Yuan-liang Ma and Wei Liu co-authored a paper and shared its presentation; thus five papers appear here for the first time in print.

Regarding the problem of translating speakers' notes or outlines into papers suitable for publication, the strategy was to ask colleagues who would not be daunted by the task to record their remarks during the presentations and prepare drafts of the papers. The following recorders labored to take down the presenters' remarks faithfully, while bringing a writer's voice to what they said: David C. Van Hoy (for Jean Hirons), Steven Miller (for Ann Huthwaite), Birdie McLennon (for Regina Romano Reynolds), and Larry Heiman (for Brian E. C. Schottlaender). In this way, these four speakers were not required to rewrite their papers, yet the readers of this volume will find material in this volume that differs from their earlier work. The speakers and their recorders worked hard together to make their papers reflect not just the words heard by the audience, but the speakers' intended meanings as well.

We have divided the work into three parts. Part 1 begins with two introductory papers: Michael Gorman's "Cataloguing in an Electronic Age" and Brian E. C. Schottlaender's "Why Metadata? Why Me? Why Now?" These papers explore, in the broadest manner, the whole topical area of libraries and metadata–why metadata should interest librarians, what role metadata might play in the larger matter of library services to individuals, and what contributions librarians might make to the development of metadata systems and their implementation in libraries.

Part 2 follows with four papers focusing on how libraries can employ metadata: Grace Agnew's "Developing a Metadata Strategy," Murtha Baca's "Practical Issues in Applying Metadata Schemas and Controlled Vocabularies to Cultural Heritage Information," Yuan-liang Ma and Wei Liu's "Digital Resources and Metadata Applications in the Shanghai Library," and Sheila S. Intner's "Struggling Toward Retrieval." The first three of these papers furnish general explanatory information about metadata systems and the principles that govern them, and describe some specific projects in which metadata was used in practice. The fourth paper takes a step back from currently accepted practices and asks whether nonstandard approaches to access for electronic resources might be more productive for the library users seeking them.

The five papers in Part 3 cover still more specific topics and include: "AACR2 and Other Metadata Standards," by Ann Huthwaite; "AACR2 and Metadata: Library Opportunities in the Global Semantic Web," by Barbara B. Tillett; "Seriality," by Jean Hirons; "MARC and Mark-Up," by Erik Jul; and "ISSN," by Regina Romano Reynolds. This group of papers deals with individual library and/or metadata standards, elements within the standards, and policies in effect at the Library of Congress. Readers should bear in mind that just as time waits for no person, some of the information discussed in the papers as "new" or "not yet accomplished" may well no longer be quite so new or may have occurred since this volume went to press. At the time the information was presented, however, the authors were correct, and efforts have been made to edit these remarks so as not to mislead anyone.

The intention of this volume is to explain, describe, and illustrate the brave new world libraries are creating through the use of metadata. It is a highly complex and dynamic world in which some things seem to shift and change constantly, and none seem to stand completely still. As editors, we have made every effort to make its contents clear and accurate. If errors appear here, we bear the full responsibility. We offer profound apologies in advance to readers of this volume as well as to the authors whose work might be affected by our mistakes. We also wish to acknowledge and applaud the incredibly hard work done by Charles Wilt, Julie Reese, and many other members of the ALCTS staff, without which the regional institutes would not have happened and this volume would not have been completed.

PART 1
FUNDAMENTALS

Cataloguing in an Electronic Age

Michael Gorman

SUMMARY. Examines the achievements in bibliographic control of the last thirty years and the strides made toward Universal Bibliographic Control. Discusses the intended and unintended effects of three standards–the MARC format, ISBD, and AACR. Analyzes the types of resources in cyberspace to be organized and their similarities to and differences from documents librarians already know. Suggests strategies for solving the seemingly insoluble problems of cataloging the Internet and predicts how metadata will evolve. *[Article copies available for a fee from The Haworth Document Delivery Service: 1-800-HAWORTH. E-mail address: <docdelivery@haworth press.com> Website: <http://www.HaworthPress.com> © 2003 by The Haworth Press, Inc. All rights reserved.]*

KEYWORDS. Cataloging standards, MARC21, AACR2R, ISBD, Universal Bibliographic Control, cataloging Web resources, metadata standards

Michael Gorman is Dean of Library Services, California State University-Fresno, 5200 North Barton, Fresno, CA 93740-8014 (E-mail: michael_gorman@csufresno.edu).

[Haworth co-indexing entry note]: "Cataloguing in an Electronic Age." Gorman, Michael. Co-published simultaneously in *Cataloging & Classification Quarterly* (The Haworth Information Press, an imprint of The Haworth Press, Inc.) Vol. 36, No. 3/4, 2003, pp. 5-17; and: *Electronic Cataloging: AACR2 and Metadata for Serials and Monographs* (ed: Sheila S. Intner, Sally C. Tseng, and Mary Lynette Larsgaard) The Haworth Information Press, an imprint of The Haworth Press, Inc., 2003, pp. 5-17. Single or multiple copies of this article are available for a fee from The Haworth Document Delivery Service [1-800-HAWORTH, 9:00 a.m. - 5:00 p.m. (EST). E-mail address: docdelivery@haworthpress.com].

10.1300/J104v36n03_02

INTRODUCTION

There is an old story about a fisherman fishing in a private river who, on being told "You can't fish here!" replied "But I am fishing here." This tale is not only illustrative of the difference between "may" and "can" that you should have learned at your mother's knee, but also of human beings' propensity not to realize that they are doing impossible things until they are told so. The impossible thing that librarians have been doing for a long time is classification–the reduction of the almost infinite dimensions of knowledge to a straight line from 000-999 or A to Z. Who but someone with the innate hubris of a cataloguer would dare to catch a flying complex subject and pin it to its exact place on that straight line to remain there forever? Now we have another impossible thing to do and we have to do it knowing that it is impossible–a thought that would never have occurred to, say, Melvil Dewey! This new impossible thing is to bring order to chaos, to trap lightning in a bottle, to take an electronic document with the life-span of a May bug (and, most likely, the cosmic significance of a May bug) and make it part of an arranged and harmonious world–in short, to apply some kind of bibliographic control to the disorder of the Internet and the Web. If there are, as politicians and futurists claim, untold intellectual riches out there in cyberspace, what use are they if they cannot be found, and found, and found again? Until we have a Networld and a Webworld with the attributes of a well-organized major library, how will we ever know if those worlds have the potential to rival Libraryworld?

The great irony of our present situation is that we have reached near-perfection in bibliographic control of "traditional" library materials at the same time as the advent of electronic resources is being seen by some as threatening the very existence of library services–including bibliographic control. Before considering the question of "cataloguing the Web and the Internet," it is salutary to review the great achievements of the past thirty years. In considering where we are going, it is necessary to know where we have been.

UNIVERSAL BIBLIOGRAPHIC CONTROL

When the ideal of Universal Bibliographic Control was first advanced[1] thirty years ago, the international library community was only beginning to discern dimly the possibilities of the interconnection of international standardization and library automation. International standardization was at a very early stage (far closer to an ideal than a reality) and the ideal of each item being catalogued once in its country of origin–the resulting record being made available to the world community–seemed far from a practical realization. Records were exchanged between countries (mostly between national libraries), but in the most inefficient manner possible–print on paper–and, since they resulted from different cataloguing codes and practices, were integrated into catalogues with great difficulty. The choice was between incorporating international records without alteration–something that degraded the catalogue very quickly–or doing such extensive revision (and retyping) that it would have been cheaper and quicker to catalogue the item oneself *ab initio.*

MAchine-Readable Cataloging (MARC) was in its infancy when Universal Bibliographic Control was proclaimed as an ideal,[2] the International Standard Bibliographic Description was still being drafted,[3] and, despite the Paris Principles,[4] cataloguing rules in different countries lacked a common basis for the assignment and form of access points ("headings"), and adhered to different descriptive practices. It was, I believe, the confluence of a need (national and research libraries throughout the world needing less expensive and more current cataloguing) and a means (automation and, more specifically, the MARC format) that has brought us nearer to Universal Bibliographic Control than anyone would have dreamed possible thirty years ago.

The idea of a universal bibliography is nearly as old as bibliography itself.[5] The idea of economies in bibliographic control by means of sharing catalogue records between libraries (cooperative cataloguing) or purchasing catalogue records for other (usually national) libraries goes back to, at least, the middle of the 19th century. In fact, the American librarian Charles Coffin Jewett drew up his cataloguing rules[6] specifically for a proposed scheme by which the Smithsonian Institution would produce "separate, stereotyped titles" to be used in the catalogues of American libraries. In these, and in the hugely successful Library of Congress catalogue card service and the *National Union Catalog* to which it gave rise, we can see bibliographic needs and desires that lacked only an appropriate technology to be met. In hindsight, it is easy to see a trajectory of inevitability that made MARC, the International Standard Bibliographic Descriptions, AACR2, and other vehicles of international bibliographic standardization seem more the result of historical forces than the often faltering and separate steps they were in truth.

BACKGROUND AND HISTORY OF THE STANDARDS

Each of the three standards I mention had original purposes that were quite different from their eventual impact on international standardization. MARC was brought into being originally to facilitate the creation of Library of Congress catalogue cards on demand. The International Standard Bibliographic Description evolved from the Standard Bibliographic Description drawn up by a committee appointed as a consequence of the International Federation of Library Associations and Institutions' International Conference of Cataloguing Experts.[7] The Standard Bibliographic Description was seen, among other things, as a means of standardizing the presentation of descriptive data so that it could be machine-translated into MARC (hence the stylized and individual punctuation). AACR2 was the culmination of decades of effort to bring uniformity to cataloguing practice in the English-speaking world, and, particularly, to reconcile British and North American descriptive cataloguing practices. Each of these three standards metamorphosed and had an impact far beyond the anticipation of all but the most far-sighted. It is instructive to recall how and why each developed and expanded, because we need to understand that the bibliographic world (just like the real world) is full of unintended consequences and the ripples from a stone thrown in one part of the bibliographic pond may eventually cover it all.

The MARC format is, by any standards, an historic achievement. It has been the main force in international standardization from a practical point of view. It is, literally, the engine that has made Universal Bibliographic Control possible. The journey from the caterpillar of the automation of card production to the beautiful butterfly of today has been long and largely successful. It is worth pointing out, however, that its origins and original purposes (including being a carrier format rather than the way in which bibliographic information is stored and manipulated) have created drawbacks that should be hardly surprising when one considers we are dealing with a thirty-year-old standard.

The structure of MARC is that of the catalogue card, when computer systems call for a different approach. Be that as it may, the fact is that there are tens of millions of MARC records in the world; MARC is accepted and used throughout the world; MARC is the basis for almost all automated bibliographic systems (including commercially produced systems); and, no practically feasible or demonstrably better system has been advocated. It should be unnecessary to point out that MARC is merely a framework standard–that is, it is a way of storing and making data capable of manipulation that has been formulated in accordance with content standards (cataloguing codes and the like). I would not trouble to point that out were it not for the frequent references to "MARC cataloguing" in writings about metadata and "simplified" cataloguing. There is, of course, no such thing as "MARC cataloguing"–MARC is the way in which we encode the results of the cataloguing process and has little or no influence on that process.

One of the two documents studied at the International Conference of Cataloguing Experts was a comparison of descriptions from cataloguing agencies throughout the world. The document revealed a great commonality of the information found in such descriptions and the order in which that information was presented. It found differences in the abbreviations used and other stylistic matters (mainly due to language differences) but was able to propose a conflation of the descriptions that formed the basis of what became the Standard Bibliographic Description and later the International Standard Bibliographic Description. Originally, the idea was to create a basis for agreement across cataloguing codes on the relatively non-contentious matter of descriptive data. Soon, however, this was supplemented by the idea that universally used distinctive punctuation, clearly identifying the areas and elements of the Standard Bibliographic Description, would not only aid in the understanding of bibliographic data in unfamiliar languages but could also be used in automatic translation of that data into MARC records. It is no coincidence that the areas and elements of the International Standard Bibliographic Description correspond exactly to the relevant fields and subfields of the MARC format. In accordance with the theme of stumbling toward standardization, it should be noted that both MARC and the International Standard Bibliographic Description were developed initially for books and only later generalized into standards for all types of library material.

The second edition of the *Anglo-American Cataloguing Rules* (AACR2) is, in fact, nothing of the sort. It was politically expedient at the time to identify this new code as a revision of the previous *Anglo-American Catalog[u]ing Rules* (1968), but AACR2 is completely different from its predecessors in several important ways. One need only cite, for instance, the facts that AACR2 is a single text (unlike its predecessors, which came in North American and British versions), is the most complete working out of the International Standard Bibliographic Description for materials of all kinds, and represents the triumph of Lubetzkian principles, which the first AACR signally did not. AACR2 quickly transcended even the historic achievement of being a unitary English-language cataloguing code to become the nearest approach to a world code we have. In the words of the introduction to the Italian translation of AACR2:[8]

> *Le Regole di catalogazione*, nella loro seconda edizione, sono il codice più diffuso nel mondo (sono state pubblicate in gran numero di lingue diverse) e l'unico che-di fatto-svolga le funzioni di codice catalografico internazionale. [The Cataloguing rules, in their second edition, are the world's most widely used (they have been translated into numerous different languages) and the only rules that are, de facto, an international cataloguing code.]

This state of affairs is partly due, of course, to the dominance of the English language (in its various manifestations) in the modern world. It is also due, in part, to the fact that AACR2 represents the most detailed working out of the principles of author/title cataloguing set forth in the Paris principles and based on the analysis and pioneering work of Seymour Lubetzky;[9] and of the application of the International Standard Bibliographic Description family of standards to all library materials.

Here we stand then, on the brink of Universal Bibliographic Control for all "traditional" (i.e., non-electronic) materials with a universally accepted format for exchanging bibliographic data, a universally accepted standard for recording descriptive data, and a quasi-universal cataloguing code that is either in use in, or influencing the codes of, most of the countries in the world. Is there any reason in principle why we should not bring electronic documents and resources into this architecture of bibliographic control? The answer is "no." Are there practical reasons why this task is formidable? The answer is "yes."

INTEGRATING ELECTRONIC DOCUMENTS

The attributes of a well-regulated library are well known to us all. They are organization, retrievability, authenticity, and stability. There are those who claim that electronic documents and sites (assemblages of electronic documents) are different in kind and not just degree from all of the other formats that human beings have used to communicate and preserve knowledge across the centuries. This is, essentially, an implausible notion—after all, at the end of the day we are still dealing with texts, images, sounds, and symbols—but its strongest support comes from the evanescence and mutability of electronic documents. Those characteristics, which any true librarian deplores, are really the logical outcome of the history of human communication–each format produces more documents than its predecessor, and each is less durable than its predecessor. It takes a long time to make many copies of stones bearing carved messages, but those messages can be read centuries later. You can send a message from Chicago to Addis Ababa in a twinkling of an eye, but that message may be expunged in a second twinkling. Many electronic documents are like those minute particles of matter that are only known because scientists can see where they have been during their micro-milliseconds of existence. Does an e-mail message exist if it is deleted unopened?

It seems to me that we should know, more precisely than we do now, exactly what it is that we are dealing with when we talk about organizing documents and sites in cyberspace. These can be divided into five types:

1. *Ephemera.* Libraries have always been far more selective than is generally acknowledged when it comes to their collections. I am not talking now of selection within formats (books, records, videos, etc.) but of ruling out, consciously or unconsciously, vast areas of recorded information. Much of the stuff that we used to ignore now shows up on the Internet and the Web. To demonstrate this, just do a search on any subject and review the few thousand "hits" with a view to imagining their tangible analogues. Personal Web pages are the electronic versions of scrapbooks and diaries–of keen interest to their compilers but to few others. Restaurant reviews? Press releases in digital form? Association newsletters? Weather forecasts? Lists of Australian university faculties? Syllabi? Advertisements? On and on it goes–acres of the cyberworld full of ephemera. What else is out there?

2. *Print-derived resources.* One useful sector of the Internet is composed of many documents and sites that are derived from the print industry and are dependent on the success of that industry for their very existence. These do not, by and large, present much of a technical problem. We know, in principle, how to catalogue different format manifestations of texts and graphic publications; thus, extending that knowledge into cyberspace is not a massive intellectual challenge. Further, print-derived electronic resources are far less transient than their purely electronic counterparts.

3. *Commercial sites and pornography.* People anxious to sell you something populate much of the electronic frontier. From e-tailers to business-to-business sites to pornographers, they are all pursuing the Great American Capitalist Dream in the sure and certain knowledge that not only is there a sucker born every minute but also that he or she is likely to spend a lot of time online.

4. *Electronic journals.* Most electronic journals are, of course, based on the products of a flourishing print industry. Forecasts over the last decade predicted that electronic journals will supplant print, but no one has, as yet, produced an economic model for such a major change and there are, at this time, a microscopic number of commercially viable true electronic journals. The problem is, of course, that the whole concept of a journal (serial assemblages of articles which are paid for in advance–whether they are ever read or not) seems inapplicable to the electronic age. Many problems in adapting to technology are caused by simply automating procedures or resources and not rethinking the whole issue. Why not, in an age of electronic communication, provide services that deliver desired articles on demand and charge the users only for the articles that they read? In such a world, the "journal" would no longer exist and libraries would be cataloguing at the level of what S. R. Ranganathan called "micro-thought"–a level that we have always left to indexing and abstracting services.

5. *Digitized archives (textual, sound, and visual).* One of the most important and valuable achievements of the electronic age is the way in which large archives have been made available to global audiences. Those archives (which are unique, by definition) have, hitherto, been accessible only to researchers with the means and time to travel to the location of the archives. To take a well-known example, the Library of Congress's *American Memory Project*[10] is a vast assemblage of pamphlets and other texts, graphic items, films, sound recordings, maps, etc., that is taking advantage of digitization and the Web to give the world access to the untold riches of the Library's archival collections. Other institutions have created Web archives of coins, stamps, posters, manuscripts, prints and drawings, early films, sound recordings, photographs, and every other conceivable means of communication, including artefacts. There has long been a great divide between library cataloguing and archival cataloguing. The former concentrates on individual manifestations of works and the latter has been largely concerned with creating finding aids for assemblages of documents. In the twenty-plus years since the appearance of AACR2, there has been some movement on this matter to bring the two cataloguing traditions closer together.[11] Although the two may always operate at different levels, there is no reason why their cataloguing practices cannot be harmonized and the results of such harmonization applied to the various parts of the *American Memory Project* and other such digital archives.

Here are the fundamental problems we encounter in trying to organize electronic documents and sites (other than those that are by-products of the print industries):

- there are too many of them
- a lot of documents and sites have never been, and never will be, of interest to libraries and library users
- the vast majority of such electronic documents are of temporary use, local use, or no use at all
- we have little or no guarantee that any given electronic document is what it says it is
- we have little or no assurance that any given document or site will be the same when next located, or that it will even exist
- there is nothing like the level of standardization of denotation and presentation that we find in books and other tangible library materials.

HISTORICAL ANTECEDENTS AND OMENS

Far from being unique, these problems are uncannily like those of manuscripts and early printed texts. The manuscript swamp from which the early printed text emerged, taking fumbling steps at first, resembles nothing so much as the electronic swamp that we now confront. We are far from the exciting world of innovation and creativity that is presented by those who hope to make money from the "information age." What we are seeing is a cultural reversion, not cultural progress. The problem with the manuscript culture was that many texts were lost, many were altered in copying, many lacked such things as titles and discernible authors, and all lacked publishers and distributors. A library burning to the ground today is a local tragedy; a library of manuscripts burning to the ground was a cultural catastrophe from which there was no recovery. Anyone who has tried to catalogue electronic documents and sites will tell you that they are elusive and shape shifting, they often lack titles and discernible authors, they may or may not exist tomorrow, they are subject to unpredictable change, and, once lost, they are lost forever. Sound familiar? There is, of course, one huge difference between the manuscript age and the looming electronic age. Pre-Gutenberg manuscripts were, by definition, created by an educated elite. Anyone doing a search using a search engine like Alta Vista is soon made painfully aware that cyberspace is littered with the productions of ignorant, semi-literate, and/or crazed individuals.

What shall we do about this reversion, this "back to the future" impending catastrophe? Those who throw their hands up in despair will surely be forgiven, but we librarians love action and will seek an answer no matter what. We need, first, to decide what it is we seek to organize. We can recognize pornography when we see it as well as any Supreme Court justice. We can recognize commercial enterprises that need no help from us in bringing themselves to the attention of potential customers. We can probably recognize the ephemeral (though one librarian's ephemeron is another's invaluable cultural resource). That still leaves us with three large classes of material–print-derived resources, digital archives, and truly electronic resources of, at least, potential value to library users. As I have said, there is no doubt that we could relatively easily bring the print-derived resources into the world system of bibliographic control using links from existing records, multi-layered records, and full records using existing standards.

Having eliminated the other slices of the electronic salami, this still leaves us with a sizeable chunk. That chunk consists of the potentially worthwhile scholarly and information resources that exist only in cyberspace and may or may not be retrievable at any given time using search engines that use free text keyword searching–well known to be the very worst information retrieval system conceived by human minds. There is something seductive about the "surfing" metaphor (especially when one remembers that surfing can be exhilarating but you end up more or less where you started, only flat on your face in the sand), but, as a Californian, I think another Golden State metaphor–panning for gold–is more apt. Are we doomed to stand in cold streams for the rest of our lives, engaged in the stoop labor of panning through the dross in ever-hopeful search of the glint of the one nugget among all the grit and stones? The answer is . . . maybe.

METADATA–THE THIRD WAY

I have gotten this far in the paper without mentioning the word "metadata," but will break that silence now. The idea behind metadata is that it is a Third Way, approximately half way between cataloguing (expensive and effective) and keyword searching (cheap and ineffective). Some believe that the future belongs to metadata–this is hard to believe given that its best-known example, the Dublin Core is an ill-formulated subset of the MARC record. Let us go back to the question of what it is that we are going to do about the worthwhile purely electronic resources that we wish to separate from the rest of the Internet and the Web. In my view, there are four possibilities. We can:

- identify and catalogue them according to standards we use for other materials
- identify them and take a subset of MARC (a framework standard, not a content standard) and call it "metadata," if that makes us feel better, to be filled with content according to bibliographic standards (either fully applied or dumbed down) by cataloguers and paraprofessionals
- identify them and take a subset of MARC and allow that framework to be filled with any content by anybody
- leave them in the murky waters of the Internet to be discovered or not discovered as determined by the karma of the searcher on the day in question.

These possibilities, obviously, range from the expensive and the effective to the inexpensive and the ineffective. There are also permutations and gradations, but those are essentially the choices before us. My belief is that "metadata," as presently conceived, will evolve toward standardization of elements and content and will be indistinguishable from real cataloguing in a relatively short time. That applies, of course, to those resources that are deemed "worthwhile." The rest will go their merry way to use, neglect, or oblivion with few tears shed.

Before we get to any kind of control, there is the question of identification of "worthwhile" materials. Again, we have choices. They are, first, a Grand Plan for cyber-collection development and, second, a grass roots movement in which individual libraries and librarians, and groups of libraries choose and catalogue the documents, resources, and sites they deem worthwhile. If you liked the drive for a national "information policy," you will love the years of striving for a national cyber-collection policy. It is not my cup of tea. The second approach will be a reprise of the history of libraries. Individuals and individual libraries built collections, one choice at a time, over many years. It was not until much later that union catalogues and library collectives brought those individual collections into a national system. The difference this time is that the benefits of the work of individual libraries and groups can be made available to all contemporaneously. Let a thousand INFOMINEs bloom, and record by record, collection by collection, "worthwhile" Internet resources will be organized and made available in what will come to be a national system following nationally-accepted standards.

CONCLUSION

Last, and most important, what is the point of all of this if the resources identified and catalogued are not preserved? Those more optimistic than I look to gigantic national electronic archives maintained by governments and private companies that will ensure the indefinite survival of the electronic records of humankind. The cost and practicalities of such schemes boggle the mind and defy credulity. We can, of course, ignore the problem and hope it all turns out right in the end–after all, that is what we are doing now. Alternatively, we could turn to the only known way of preserving massive numbers of texts and images–print them on acid-free paper. If you are inclined to laugh at that suggestion, I would recommend that you explore the financial costs and the cultural costs of the alternatives, and keep an open mind.

Metadata is a buzzword that is losing its buzziness, but real problems and real issues lurk behind all the pomposity and techno-babble. What are we going to do about identifying and making accessible the valuable records of humanity that are only available in electronic form? How are we going to deal with the mutability and evanescence of those records? How are we going to preserve those resources and transmit them to posterity? We will only answer these questions if we employ wisdom and insight, are cognizant of the lessons of history, and work with the interests of all our users, present and future, in mind.

AUTHOR NOTE

Michael Gorman is Dean of Library Services at the Henry Madden Library, California State University, Fresno. From 1977 to 1988 he worked at the University of Illinois, Urbana, Library as, successively, Director of Technical Services, Director of General Services, and Acting University Librarian. From 1966 to 1977 he was, successively, Head of Cataloguing at the *British National Bibliography*, a member of the British Library Planning Secretariat, and Head of the Office of Bibliographic Standards in the British Library. He has taught at library schools in his native Britain and in the United States–most recently as Visiting Professor at the University of California, Berkeley, School of Library and Information Science (summer sessions).

He is the first editor of the *Anglo-American Cataloguing Rules, Second Edition* (1978) and of the revision of that work (1988). He is the author of *The Concise AACR2*, 3rd edition (1999); editor of, and contributor to, *Technical Services Today and Tomorrow*, 2nd edition (1998); and editor of *Convergence* (proceedings of 2nd National LITA Conference), and *Californien*, both published in 1991. *Future Libraries: Dreams, Madness, and Reality*, co-written with Walt Crawford, was honored with the 1997 Blackwell's Scholarship Award. He published *Our Singular Strengths* in 1997. His most recent book, *Our Enduring*

Values, published by ALA in 2000, was the winner of ALA's 2001 Highsmith award for the best book on librarianship. Mr. Gorman is the author of hundreds of articles in professional and scholarly journals. He has contributed chapters to a number of books and is the author or editor of other books and monographs. He has given numerous presentations at international, national, and state conferences.

Michael Gorman is a fellow of the [British] Library Association, the 1979 recipient of the Margaret Mann Citation, the 1992 recipient of the Melvil Dewey Medal, the 1997 recipient of Blackwell's Scholarship Award, and the 1999 recipient of the California Library Association/Access, Collections, and Technical Services Section Award of Achievement.

REFERENCES

1. Kaltwasser, Franz Georg, "Universal Bibliographic Control," *Unesco Library Bulletin* 25 (September 1971): 252-259.

2. Avram, Henriette, "The Evolving MARC System: The Concept of a Data Utility," In *Clinic on Library Applications of Data Processing, 1970* (Urbana, Ill.: University of Illinois, 1971), pp. 1-26.

3. Gorman, Michael, "Standard Bibliographic Description," *Catalogue & Index* 22 (Summer 1971): 3-5.

4. Chaplin, A.H., "Cataloguing Principles: Five Years after the Paris Conference," *Unesco Library Bulletin* 21 (May 1967): 140-145.

5. Gesner, Konrad, 1516-1565. *Biblioteca universalis, sive, Catalogus omnium scriptorum locupletissimus, in tribus linguis, latina, graeca, & hebraica* (Zurich: Apud Christoph Froschauer, 1545).

6. Jewett, Charles Coffin [1816-1868] *On the Construction of Catalogues of Libraries, and their Publication by Means of Separate, Stereotyped Titles*, 2nd ed. (Washington: Smithsonian Institution, 1853).

7. "Report of the International Meeting of Cataloguing Experts, Copenhagen," *Libri* 20, nos. 1-2 (1970): 105-137.

8. *Regole di catalogazione Angloamericane*, 2. ed., revisione del 1988. (Editrice bibliografica, 1997), p. vii.

9. *The Future of Cataloging: Insights from the Lubetzky Symposium*, (Chicago: ALA, 2000).

10. Available at <http://memory.loc.gov/>.

11. See, for example, Hensen, Steven. "NISTFII and EAD: The Evolution of Archival Description," *American Archivist* 60, no. 3 (1998): 284-296.

Why Metadata?
Why Me?
Why Now?

Brian E. C. Schottlaender

SUMMARY. Provides an introductory overview to the subject of metadata, which considers why metadata issues are central to discussions about the evolution of library services–particularly digital library services–and why the cataloging community is, and should be, front and center in those discussions. *[Article copies available for a fee from The Haworth Document Delivery Service: 1-800-HAWORTH. E-mail address: <docdelivery@haworthpress. com> Website: <http://www.HaworthPress.com> © 2003 by The Haworth Press, Inc. All rights reserved.]*

KEYWORDS. Metadata standards, cataloging community, encoding schema, content standards

There is a young woman who works in my office and is responsible for taking minutes at various meetings that take place within the University of California San Diego Libraries, including those of the library management group we simply call "The Cabinet." She had been doing her work beautifully for many months when she approached my deputy

Brian E. C. Schottlaender is University Librarian, University of California-San Diego, 9500 Gilman Drive 0175G, La Jolla, CA 92093-0175 (E-mail: becs@ucsd. edu).

This article was transcribed by Larry Heiman, Head, Copy Cataloging Team, University of California-Irvine.

[Haworth co-indexing entry note]: "Why Metadata? Why Me? Why Now?" Schottlaender, Brian E. C. Co-published simultaneously in *Cataloging & Classification Quarterly* (The Haworth Information Press, an imprint of The Haworth Press, Inc.) Vol. 36, No. 3/4, 2003, pp. 19-29; and: *Electronic Cataloging: AACR2 and Metadata for Serials and Monographs* (ed: Sheila S. Intner, Sally C. Tseng, and Mary Lynette Larsgaard) The Haworth Information Press, an imprint of The Haworth Press, Inc., 2003, pp. 19-29. Single or multiple copies of this article are available for a fee from The Haworth Document Delivery Service [1-800-HAWORTH, 9:00 a.m. - 5:00 p.m. (EST). E-mail address: docdelivery@haworthpress.com].

10.1300/J104v36n03_03

one day and asked, "What is this meetadata [sic] I keep hearing about?" I thought about calling my talk this morning, "So What's Up With Metadata?" but decided instead to pose the three title questions–"Why metadata? Why me? Why now?"–as a means of providing an introductory overview and framework for the presentations to follow. I intend, at the end of my presentation, to answer the three questions; but first, I want to use them as a means of framing what I hope will be a useful overview of both the information environment and the professional environment in which we find ourselves.

WHY METADATA?

If anything characterizes the information universe in which we find ourselves today, it is its fluidity. There are a proliferating number of information resources, a number of which serve highly specialized needs. Many of these resources are complex and packaged in such a way that their individual components may actually require management. These characteristics of the information universe inform the characteristics of the metadata environment as well.

As we all know, there probably are as many definitions of metadata as there are people whom one asks. In fact, when the Task Force on Metadata summarized the various definitions they came across in the course of their work in an appendix to its Final Report,[1] they included well over 25 of them. One of the best was Clifford Lynch's: "a cloud of collateral information around a data object."[2] What I like about this definition is its use of the words "cloud" and "collateral." "Cloud" evokes for me that character in Peanuts who always had that cloud of dirt all around him, while "collateral" makes clear the inherent relationship between data and their metadata. The Task Force used the definitions found in the environment to craft their own. In many ways, I believe theirs still is the best of the formal definitions of metadata that exist, with Lynch's standing as the best informal definition. The Task Force definition is this: metadata are "structured, encoded data that describe characteristics of information-bearing entities to aid in the identification, discovery, assessment, and management of the described entities."[3] Whether one considers metadata to be structured data that describe the characteristics of a resource or clouds of collateral information around data, there is an inherent relationship between metadata and the information objects they describe.

Having said earlier that one of the characteristics of the information environment in which we find ourselves is a proliferating number of resources, the corollary to that is: metadata, metadata everywhere. Also, having said earlier that the resources in the digital information environment in which we find ourselves are increasingly specialized, increasingly fluid, and increasingly complex, the implication on the metadata side is that metadata are having to do more and more things.

A word one hears a lot in discussions of metadata is the word "schema." There are many definitions of that word as well, including that it is just a fancy word for scheme. The most useful that I've come across thus far is Murtha Baca's in her *Introduction to Metadata*, edited for the Getty Research Institute. She defines schema quite usefully as "a set of rules for encoding information that supports specific communities of users."[4] There are three kinds of schema I want to talk about: encoding schema; metadata schema; and architectural schema.

Encoding Schema

Encoding schema are many; but the four I want to mention are MARC, SGML, HTML, and XML. MARC (MAchine Readable Cataloging), with which we are arguably the most familiar, is the standard structure for encoding cataloging data, most often bibliographic and authority data, though there are other applications. SGML (Standard Generalized Markup Language) is an international standard, ISO 8879, that prescribes a format for embedding descriptive markup within a document and then goes on to specify a method for describing the structure of that document. SGML basically has three claims to fame: extensibility; structuring capabilities; and, validation capabilities. SGML is crafted in such a way that it allows one to deal with the complex package resources mentioned earlier. It allows one to do so in a highly structured fashion and to do it in such a way that one can validate the structure as the markup is taking place. Those are its upsides; it has downsides as well. It is extremely complex and applying it demands, frankly, a rigor that many of us don't care to invest. The markup language with which most people are more familiar and more comfortable is HTML (HyperText Markup Language). There is a widespread perception and, frankly, it is a misperception, that HTML is "dumbed-down" SGML. In fact, while HTML is based on SGML, it is not a subset of it, though the people who created it definitely had SGML in mind when they did so. HTML is intended for marking up hypertext, multimedia, and reasonably small, simple documents. The most recent markup language being talked about in our community is XML (Extensible Markup Language), conceived basically as a happy medium, if you will, between HTML and SGML. In fact, XML is a simplified subset of SGML intended for Web applications. It retains SGML's extensibility as is implied by its name, along with SGML's structure and validation capabilities, but it is much simpler to apply.

Metadata Schema

The number of metadata types is proliferating as the resources metadata are intended to manage proliferate as well. Whereas once upon a time long ago–say, five years ago–when people talked about metadata and how complex the world of metadata was, they were usually talking about four basic types: descriptive; administrative; technical; and rights metadata. Now, there are now a good many more, including: security; personal information (for example, Vcard); commercial management (cost, etc.); content rating; and preservation metadata. I shall focus primarily on descriptive metadata, reviewing several of the schema being used in the descriptive metadata community.

In the library cataloging community, ISBD (International Standard Bibliographic Description) is the widely adopted schema for describing many types of library materials. The *Anglo-American Cataloguing Rules*, second edition (AACR2), meanwhile, is a content standard for bibliographic data relating to library materials and for formulating access points for authors, titles, related works, etc. The Program for Cooperative Cataloging (PCC) core record standards, of which there are now almost a dozen for everything from books to multiple character sets, is another. All are MARC-based descriptive metadata schema.

The non-cataloging community descriptive metadata schema familiar to most of us is Dublin Core (known officially as the "Dublin Metadata Core Element Set"). It is, as its name implies, a core set of elements, a simple set of data elements, meant to be used to describe and facilitate discovery of document-like objects in a networked environment. That phrase "document-like objects" is important, because the digital information universe is full of digital objects that are not document-like and Dublin Core may or may not be useful in describing them.

In the government documents community, metadata schema in use include AGLS, which stands for Australian Government Locator Service, a Dublin Core-based descriptive schema. Another is FGDC, a metadata standard developed by the Federal Geographic Data Committee for digital geospatial metadata. It, in turn, is based on the Content Standard for Digital Geospatial Metadata (known as CSDGM), an XML-based metadata standard.

In the art community, the REACH (Record Export for Art and Cultural Heritage) Element Set is a metadata standard elements set developed by the Research Libraries Group. The core elements in the set are drawn from various standards in the cultural heritage and art environments, including the CDWA (Categories for the Descriptions of Works of Art), the Data Dictionary created by MESL (the Museum Educational Site Licensing project), and the Access Points crafted by the Consortium for the Computer Interchange of Museum Information (CIMI). The REACH Element Set is interesting because it functions as a meta-metadata set to the extent that it incorporates a variety of data elements from other metadata standards. The VRA Core Categories, meanwhile, is a metadata elements set created by the Visual Resources Association Data Standards Committee to describe visual resources and the images that describe them.

Two other important descriptive schema are the Text Encoding Initiative (TEI) and EAD (Encoded Archival Description) Headers. Both TEI and EAD are document types within SGML. Their headers, in turn, are those sets of elements within their respective document-type definitions designed to contain identifying data about instances of each. Both function, in effect, as metadata supersets.

Two non-descriptive metadata schema I want to mention just briefly are PICS and A'Core. PICS (Platform for Internet Content Selectivity) was one of the first and remains one of the most robust content rating initiatives. PICS metadata are instrumental in a commercial search engine's ability to allow one to restrict access to certain kinds of Internet content. A'Core (Admin Core) is a metadata standard for metadata. Systems use A'Core metadata "to determine the currency and integrity of content metadata, and provide details on how to contact entities involved with the management of content metadata."[5] In the increasingly complex systems within which we are working, multiple metadata standards or schema are at work managing different kinds of objects. It is the Admin Core that helps systems keep track of all these metadata.

A word now about "identifiers," a highly concentrated kind of descriptive metadata: The International Standard Book Number (ISBN) and International Standard Serial Number (ISSN) are probably the most familiar identifiers to librarians. ISAN, the International Standard Audiovisual Number, is perhaps less so. Beyond these are a variety of URIs, or Uniform Resource Identifiers, the most familiar of which is the URL (Uniform Resource Locator) that characteristically begins "http://." Other types of URIs include URNs and URCs, or Uniform Resource Names and Uniform Resource Characteristics, respectively. Both are intended to function much the same way as URLs do, but obviate some of the problems that URLs have, including, most notably, the propensity to change regularly. Those who are working on URN and URC development hope that names and characteristics are more constant than locations. Whether that is so remains to be seen.

With some exceptions, the descriptive metadata schema just described generally focus on syntax. Semantics has remained the domain of library cataloging, notably as manifest in AACR2. In other words, many metadata schema focus on statements like, "When you describe an object, you should be sure to include in that description its title, creator, etc." The schema rarely go on to tell one how to do that. Instead, it is the library cataloging community, and its AACR2, that have focused on deciding whether an object has a title or a creator and, if so, how to formulate them.

Architectural Schema

Having talked a little bit about a variety of descriptive schema, let me now talk about three architectural schema. The first, Interoperability of Data in E-Commerce Systems (INDECS), is important in part because of who created it. It was established to integrate a variety of standards developed by communities that concern themselves with copyright, including the copyright societies' Common Information System (CIS) plan, the record industry's International Standard Recording Code (ISRC) and MUSE projects, the audiovisual community's International Standard Audiovisual Number (ISAN) initiative, the publishing industry's ISBN and ISSN initiatives, and the Digital Objective Identifier (DOI) initiative.[6]

In our community, the two architectural schema we are more likely to have heard of are RDF (the Resource Description Framework) and the Warwick Framework. RDF is an infrastructure for "encoding, exchange, and reuse of structured metadata."[7] The Warwick Framework extends that concept to some extent, and is defined as "a container architecture for diverse sets of metadata."[8] In other words, it is a comprehensive infrastructure for network resource description. At University of California San Diego's Supercomputer Center, computer scientists have developed something called the Storage Resource Broker, or SRB, which is predicated on the Warwick Framework. It is a software suite that allows one to pull a variety of digital objects into a container architecture that can handle basically any kind of metadata. The container architecture really does not care what metadata schema was used to encode the data because it manages everything at a kind of super ordinary architectural level.

WHY ME?

Let me talk a little bit now about the second question, "Why me?" Why should catalogers be in the forefront of metadata development? Metadata is about access. Cataloging is about access. Cataloging describes content and content relationships. Kevin Butterfield talks about cataloging as an "invisible process of order-making."[9] At the risk of stating the obvious, the Internet could use some order-making. Cataloging, Butterfield points out and we all know intuitively, is not about rules; nor is it about the records created as a result of those rules. It is about standards; it is about vocabulary development; and it is about the development of systems for description and classification. These are processes the cataloging community has been involved in for a long, long time–decades, if not centuries–and we have a lot of experience and expertise to offer other communities who think that these issues are only now being considered for the first time. The report of the Task Force on Metadata and the Cataloging Rules stated that "Catalogers need to be involved with emerging metadata standards. Our bibliographic and cataloging expertise is invariably useful and often welcome in defining data elements and preparing usage guidelines."[10] I'm not sure that "often welcome" was true in 1998. Now, four years later, I think it is much more accurate.

In the Task Force report, co-author John Attig observed that the intersection between cataloging and metadata is, or should be, the common user tasks they support.[11] The International Federation of Library Associations and Institutions' *Functional Requirements for Bibliographic Records* (FRBR) describes these common user tasks as fourfold: find, select, identify, and obtain.[12] I suspect that when Attig uses the word "common" he is using it in two ways. First of all, the tasks themselves are common; second, they are common to a very broad spectrum of users. Cataloging and metadata, I would suggest, intersect in the degree to which they support these tasks.

WHY NOW?

Earlier, I noted that most metadata schema have focused on syntax rather than semantics. Putting it another way, most, if not all, content standards are library-based: AACR2, *Art & Architecture Thesaurus* (AAT), *Library of Congress Subject Headings* (LCSH), *Archives, Personal Papers, and Manuscripts* (APPM). They all came out of the library community. Very few, if any, content standards exist outside the library community. It is my perception, apropos of the 1998 observation that catalogers' expertise is often welcome, that the initial non-library ambivalence, if not outright hostility, to content standard development is beginning to evaporate. There is a growing recognition in the non-library community of the utility and desirability of content standards. In fact, I see an increasing confluence between the cataloging and metadata communities, so much so, that the two communities are becoming harder to distinguish, which is exactly as it should be. Consider, for instance, the following words from Stuart Weibel: "The 15 Dublin Core elements might be more coherently expressed if they are related to an underlying logical model such as that expressed in the Functional Requirements for Bibliographic Records (FRBR) of the International Federation of Library Associations."[13] Coming from the same person who had earlier put the Dublin Core forward as an alternative to cataloging, the statement approaches revelation. The Dublin Core "qualifiers" you may have heard about are, basically, an attempt being made now to enrich the Dublin Core Element Set by referencing a variety of content standards: subject thesauri; authority control systems; and classification systems.

On the one hand, there is a growing recognition in the metadata community of the relevance of the work that we in the library cataloging community have been doing. On the other, commercial and legal interests in rights management, with which the library community is deeply concerned, may bring the communities even closer together, if for no other reason than the fact that rights management requires a degree of descriptive specificity that is characteristically practiced, thus far at least, by the cataloging community and not by the metadata community. Put in FRBR terms, whereas the focus of the metadata community has been on "find" and "obtain," the "identify" task, which is essential to effective rights management, has been the focus of much greater effort within the cataloging community. The Task Force on Metadata and the Cataloging Rules stated: "Our catalogs have become one tool among many, but those many are not separate or isolated from one another. The catalog is one tool in a network of tools."[14]

CONCLUSION

I want to conclude by talking a little about the challenges and opportunities that the environment holds now for us in the metadata and cataloging communities. A significant challenge is that of the degree of "fixity," or lack thereof, of e-documents. Fixity is a concept most recently articulated by David Levy of the University of Washington's library school faculty to refer to how fixed in time and space documents are. Levy observes that in a print environment documents are much more fixed in time and space than they are in a digital environment.[15] I suggest the degree to which electronic documents are not fixed in time and space has serious implications for the necessarily dynamic nature of the metadata associated with those documents.

Another challenge is that of content standards. While it is true there is a growing confluence between the cataloging and metadata communities, an incredible amount of work remains to be done on content standards and, related to it, on controlled vocabulary sets. Development of the latter becomes particularly complex when it needs to take place across different sectors of the content community. The vocabulary set that the art and architecture community finds comfortable is going to be quite different from that of the social sciences community. Consistent deployment of metadata across variant content communities will be a challenge, as will harmonization (a word I prefer to "compatibility") of metadata sets.

Perhaps more than anything, interoperability issues will be challenging. Interoperability is defined as "the ability of two or more systems or components to exchange information and use the exchanged information without special effort on either system."[16] When the communities talk about interoperability, they invariably mean syntactic, semantic, and structural interoperability. These are challenging technical issues to be sure. Equally challenging, however, are the cultural interoperability issues that persist between the communities themselves.

To return to my three questions–"Why metadata? Why me? Why now?"–I respond to them by saying, "Because it is inescapable and seemingly more evident every day; because it is what we are about; and finally, because not only do we need metadata as another tool in our network of tools to do what we do, but metadata needs us to help fully realize its potential."

AUTHOR NOTE

Brian E. C. Schottlaender has been University Librarian at the University of California, San Diego (UCSD) since September 1999. Prior to joining UCSD, his twenty-plus year career in libraries included positions at the California Digital Library, UCLA, the University of Arizona, Indiana University, and Harrassowitz in Wiesbaden, Germany, one of Europe's oldest and most respected library booksellers and subscription agents.

A member of the American Library Association (ALA) since 1979, Mr. Schottlaender has served on the Board of Directors of ALA's Association for Library Collections and Technical Services since 1996. From 1995 to 2001, he served as the ALA Representative to the international Joint Steering Committee for Revision of the Anglo-American Cataloguing Rules. In 1997 and 1998, he chaired the Program for Cooperative Cataloging at the Library of Congress. From 1999 through 2001 he served as Chair of the Pacific Rim Digital Alliance, and since 1999 he has chaired the San Diego Library Circuit. In 2001, he was elected to the Board of Directors of the Association of Research Libraries, an organization comprising the leading research libraries in the United States and Canada.

Mr. Schottlaender has edited two books: *The Future of the Descriptive Cataloging Rules: Proceedings of the AACR 2000 Preconference* (1998) and *Retrospective Conversion: History, Approaches, Considerations* (1992). He has contributed articles to various professional journals, including *Rare Books and Manuscripts Librarianship* and *Journal of Internet Cataloging*, and has spoken widely on collections, bibliographic access, and digital library issues.

Mr. Schottlaender obtained his BA degree in German Studies from the University of Texas, Austin in 1974 (*ampla cum laude*). He received his MS degree in Library Science from Indiana University in 1980, the same year he was admitted to Beta Phi Mu, the Library Science Honor Society. In 1995, he was one of fifteen individuals selected nationally to attend the Palmer School of Library Science at Long Island University as a Senior Fellow. Mr. Schottlaender is the 2001 recipient of the Margaret Mann Citation from the American Library Association for outstanding professional achievement in cataloging and classification.

REFERENCES

1. Association for Library Collections & Technical Services, Committee on Cataloging: Description and Access, Task Force on Metadata, *Final Report* (June 2000). Available at <http://www.ala.org/alcts/organization/ccs/ccda/tf-meta6.html>.

2. Ibid.

3. Ibid.

4. Baca, Murtha, ed., *Introduction to Metadata*, Los Angeles: Getty Research Institute, 1998. Available at <http://getty.edu/research/institute/standards/intrometadata/>.

5. Iannella, Renato and Debbie Campbell, "The A-Core: Metadata about Content Metadata," (Internet-Draft, 30 June 1999). Available at <http://metadata.net/admin/draft-iannella-admin-01.txt>.

6. Bearman, David, Eric Miller, Godfrey Rust, Jennifer Trant, and Stuart Weibel, "A Common Model to Support Interoperable Metadata: Progress Report on Reconciling Metadata Requirements from the Dublin Core and INDECS/DOI Communities," *D-Lib Magazine* (January 1999). Available at <http://www.dlib.org/dlib/january99/bearman/01bearman.html>.

7. Miller, Eric, "An Introduction to the Resource Description Framework," *D-Lib Magazine* (May 1998). Available at <http://www.dlib.org/dlib/may98/miller/05miller.html>.

8. Lagoze, Carl, "The Warwick Framework: A Container Architecture for Diverse Sets of Metadata," *D-Lib Magazine* (July/August 1996). Available at <http://www.dlib.org/dlib/july96/lagoze/07lagoze.html>.

9. Butterfield, Kevin, "Catalogers and the Creation of Metadata Systems," available at <http://www.oclc.org/oclc/man/colloq/butter.htm>.

10. Association for Library Collections & Technical Services, Committee on Cataloging: Description and Access, Task Force on Metadata and the Cataloging Rules, *Final Report* (August 1998). Available at <http://www.ala.org/alcts/organization/ccs/ccda/tf-tei2.html>.

11. Ibid.

12. IFLA Study Group on the Functional Requirements for Bibliographic Records. *Functional Requirements for Bibliographic Records: Final Report.* Munchen: K.G. Saur, 1998.

13. Weibel, Stuart, "The State of the Dublin Core Metadata Initiative," *D-Lib Magazine* (April 1999). Available at: <http://www.dlib.org/dlib/april99/04weibel.html>.

14. Association for Library Collections & Technical Services. Committee on Cataloging: Description and Access. Task Force on Metadata, *Final Report* (June 2000). <http://www.ala.org/alcts/organization/ccs/ccda/tf-meta6.html>.

15. Levy, David, "Fixed or Fluid? Document Stability and New Media," In *Proceedings of the 1994 European Conference on Hypermedia Technology* (ACM Press, 1994), p. 24-31.

16. Association for Library Collections & Technical Services, Committee on Cataloging: Description and Access, Task Force on Metadata, *Final Report* (June 2000). Available at <http://www.ala.org/alcts/organization/ccs/ccda/tf-meta6.html>.

PART 2
HOW LIBRARIES
CAN EMPLOY METADATA

Developing a Metadata Strategy

Grace Agnew

SUMMARY. This paper covers the steps in building a metadata repository, including modeling the information needs of your community, selecting and adapting a metadata standard, documenting your metadata, populating the database, and sharing your metadata with other repositories and metadata initiatives. In addition, advances and options that can be applied to metadata for multimedia, particularly video, are presented. *[Article copies available for a fee from The Haworth Document Delivery Service: 1-800-HAWORTH. E-mail address: <docdelivery@haworthpress.com> Website: <http://www.HaworthPress.com> © 2003 by The Haworth Press, Inc. All rights reserved.]*

KEYWORDS. Metadata standards, catalog databases, metadata initiatives, multimedia, video/moving image

Grace Agnew is Associate University Librarian for Digital Library Services, Technical Services Building, Rutgers University Libraries, 47 Davidson Road, Piscataway, NJ 08854-5603 (E-mail: gagnew@rci.rutgers.edu).

[Haworth co-indexing entry note]: "Developing a Metadata Strategy." Agnew, Grace. Co-published simultaneously in *Cataloging & Classification Quarterly* (The Haworth Information Press, an imprint of The Haworth Press, Inc.) Vol. 36, No. 3/4, 2003, pp. 31-46; and: *Electronic Cataloging: AACR2 and Metadata for Serials and Monographs* (ed: Sheila S. Intner, Sally C. Tseng, and Mary Lynette Larsgaard) The Haworth Information Press, an imprint of The Haworth Press, Inc., 2003, pp. 31-46. Single or multiple copies of this article are available for a fee from The Haworth Document Delivery Service [1-800-HAWORTH, 9:00 a.m. - 5:00 p.m. (EST). E-mail address: docdelivery@haworthpress.com].

http://www.haworthpress.com/store/product.asp?sku=J104
© 2003 by The Haworth Press, Inc. All rights reserved.
10.1300/J104v36n03_04

31

DEVELOPING A METADATA STRATEGY

Metadata can be simply defined as data about data. In the traditional library setting, metadata resides in a library's catalog and describes information resources collected or managed by the library. In the digital information age, however, metadata has truly come into its own. Metadata brings intelligence and coherence to digital collections, as well as order and meaning to the fragmented Web. Metadata can be used to document every facet of a digital library initiative: selection, organization, preservation, discovery, and interpretation of digital information.

MARC (MAchine Readable Cataloging) was a tremendous breakthrough in the evolution of metadata. MARC adhered to well-documented formatting principles–the *Anglo-American Cataloguing Rules* and International Standard Bibliographic Description (ISBD) punctuation–to create coherent, interoperable metadata that could be shared and interpreted by an international community. At the time of this writing, MARC remains the most mature metadata standard available.

In recent years, new metadata systems, called "schemas," have evolved, generally geared to an information format, such as Encoded Archival Description (EAD); designed for archival finding aids for a community of users, such as CIDOC (Le Comite international pour la documentation du Conseil international des musees); or for an information medium, such as TEI (Text Encoding Initiative) for text, and MPEG-7 (Motion Picture Experts Group) for multimedia information. XML-based schemas to describe and document different types of digital information, including musical notation, mathematical equations, and electronic journals, among others, have also appeared. Many of the schemas incorporate descriptive metadata in the header or the body of the XML document. Libraries have many choices and options for rich description of digital resources.

Despite an abundance of tools and technologies for describing and managing digital objects, what is lacking is a road map to a coherent metadata strategy. How does a library decide how to invest its scarce human resources to best serve its primary user population? Metadata was much simpler and the opportunities for costly error less abundant when the only question was how, for example, how to implement MARC. Now the questions are more complex, asking also what to implement and why.

A good metadata strategy should possess the following five qualities, and be:

- *Scalable.* Having a flexible design that supports changing user needs and new technologies.
- *Standardized.* Shareable by users and metadata registries worldwide.
- *Unambiguous.* The information contained within the metadata should provide for consistent, unique interpretation by human and machine users.
- *Effective.* The metadata must persist over space and time, be readily accessible to users and integrate tightly with the information resources it describes.
- *Integrated.* The metadata must integrate with legacy metadata, such as the library's primary catalog, to present uniform and consistent description and management of the library's information resources.

Metadata may be intrinsic to the digital object, such as the header information in a TEI-encoded text, extrinsic to the digital object, such as the metadata stored in a centralized database, or a combination of the two strategies. An example of a combination strategy would be the harvesting of intrinsic metadata from the digital object into a centralized database. Metadata can be automatically generated, particularly from intelligent digital objects, such as XML-structured documents, or human-created. What is most important, however, is that metadata is based on the needs of the primary user base and represents a solid understanding of the user's information universe. An effective metadata standard will be designed to locate the information object within the user's information universe, so that the information object makes contextual sense within the user's overall information needs.

The first step–and the most difficult–is to truly understand the information universe of the primary customer base. This information universe can be understood and documented as a basic model consisting of entities, relationships among entities and attributes of entities. The primary entities involved are the user; the metadata creator, particularly in relationship to the user; the metadata that enables discovery and evaluation of information; and the digital information objects that are being described, discovered and used within the information environment.

The information universe involves the constraints on the user that dictate what information is needed and how it is used. Common constraints include knowledge domains, such as astrophysics or medicine; organizations, such as a university or a company; and the user's application needs for information, such as research, teaching, or industrial needs. It is critical to look beyond the primary domain to related or "edge" domains. A university may be part of a consortium, for example, or may be collaborating with another university in offering distance education courses. A study of student citations on research papers may indicate a heavy reliance on general Web resources, discovered via an Internet search engine, as opposed to the library's collection. It is important to use metadata to integrate the digital collections described and made accessible by the library into the larger information domain of the customer.

A flexible metadata strategy will involve an understanding of the changing needs and roles of the user. Web-based search engines such as Google and Alta Vista have become simpler to use but increasingly sophisticated in their processing and data mining capabilities. Users have come to expect that information discovery and retrieval will be fast, contextual, customized to their unique needs, and accurate. User roles are also evolving, as Web publishing becomes simpler to employ. A typical academic user is an information seeker, an information publisher, and also a lifelong learner, as graduates in the commercial world struggle to keep up with rapidly changing technologies and expanding knowledge bases in every field. It is impossible to grasp effectively and utilize the exploding information core in any field–the humanities and social sciences as well as medicine and the sciences.

THE INFORMATION MODEL

One begins an information model by understanding the user base, the information domains, and the information seeking behaviors of the users. One can conduct interviews and surveys, and study usage logs for the library's digital information sources. A good way to understand users' information needs is to examine end products. In the university setting, this may be the textbooks and materials placed on course reserves; the books, articles, term papers, theses and dissertations produced by faculty and students; the grants for which members of the university have applied; and the digital information faculty and students have self-published on the Web.

A basic model of the academic information universe and the role of metadata in that universe looks something like Illustration A.

Once the primary entities within the model are understood–the users and the information resources they employ–one is ready to develop a metadata system to support their needs for discovery, evaluation, access, and for information with persistent accuracy and integrity.

A metadata system will include the all the components in the architecture diagram shown in Illustration B.

ILLUSTRATION A

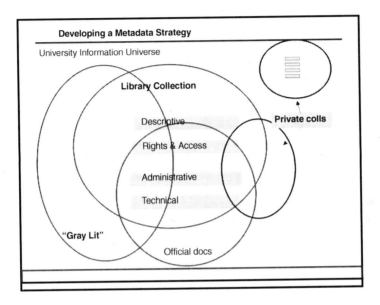

ILLUSTRATION B

METADATA SCHEMA COMPONENTS

- **Data Element** - Atomic Unit of Meaning - Community Defined
- **Attribute** - Refines, Extends, Interprets data element
- **Value** - Information unique to each data element instance
- **Constraint** - Order imposed on data element expression for consistency; semantic viability
- **Label** - contextual instance of data element name. "How the data element displays on the Web for the end user."

The metadata system will be based on the information model that represents one's best understanding of the users, their information domain, and how they gather and use information resources. Based on the needs of the user population, one selects a primary metadata schema to serve as the sole metadata schema or, as I recommend, as a "root" schema, to which other schema can be appended as extensions based on the needs of the subject, the user, or the resource itself.

Selecting and implementing a root schema can enable metadata format independence, since a good root schema will map readily, and thus be subsumed readily, within schemas with more extensive elements or schemas that are customized for particular subjects or formats, such as the geospatial standard, CSGDM (Content Standard for Digital Geospatial Metadata, more commonly known as "FDGC"). Two other root schemas worth serious consideration are MARC and Dublin Core.

MARC has been revised a number of times and is currently called MARC 21, a version edited at the turn of the 21st century. MARC is a mature, well-maintained standard with prescribed formatting rules and controlled vocabularies for every element. MARC is found in library catalogs around the world and is readily shared and interpreted by integrated library management systems and library users worldwide. Much community effort has been expended to develop core MARC profiles, particularly the Program for Cooperative Cataloging's MARC core record. MARC maps readily to many metadata schemas, or perhaps more accurately, most metadata standards have developed mappings to this pre-eminent legacy standard.

Dublin Core, which consists of fifteen optional, repeatable elements, is more properly an element set than a schema. In fact, developers and proponents of Dublin Core rarely agree on whether Dublin Core is a true schema or not. However, even in its unqualified element set form, it has been used by many digital library initiatives and consortia as a schema. The Computer Interchange of Museum Information (CIMI) consortium is one that has developed an application profile for all fifteen optional, repeatable elements, to great effect. Dublin Core is a good choice for a root schema because it was developed primarily to support mapping among schemas, because it supports data sharing initiatives such as the Open Archives Initiative protocol, and because it was designed for simplicity of use so it can enable collaboration with digital publishers and creators who are not metadata specialists.

Implementing a core or root schema implies that one's organization will be developing an application profile for the schema. A core schema is frequently a distillation of the most critical elements from a much more complex schema, such as MARC or, in the case of an existing core schema, such as Dublin Core, so the application profile will impose order and constraints on unconstrained data elements. Developing the application profile for one's root schema is one of the most important components of metadata system development.

COMPONENTS OF A METADATA SCHEMA

Before developing an application profile, it is important to understand the parts of a metadata schema, as expressed within a single unit describing an information object–the metadata record. The atomic element of a data record, that is, the smallest unit of independent semantic meaning, is the data element. The data element, often expressed as a field or subfield within a metadata record, is considered an atomic element, but the truth is that irreducible (or atomic) semantic meaning is determined by the metadata developers. An atomic element can be as broad or as specific as the needs of the community dictate. For example, "place of publication" can be a data element for one community, and the formatting rules can allow "city," "state," "country," or any combination of the three elements expressed in a free-text format. Alternatively, metadata for another community, such as a book distributor or book seller community, might be much more specific, with "city of publication," "state of publication," and "country of publication" each required as separate data elements with controlled vocabularies and precise formatting rules for each element.

It is not critical to develop data elements to some abstract principle of atomic distillation so much as it is critical that data elements conform to three basic principles:

1. the data elements have meaning and are useful to the primary user community;
2. the data elements are well-developed with definitions, formatting principles, and controlled vocabularies, to enable interpretation and sharing by human and computer users;
3. the data elements are well-documented in a data registry.

The next component of a metadata schema is the rules that apply to each data element. These rules include the primary constraints: whether a data element is optional, mandatory, or recommended; whether a data element is repeatable; and the recommended or required order of appearance in the metadata record.

The next component of a metadata schema is the attributes of each data element, which are primarily "type," "role" (for agents, such as creators, contributors and publishers), "label," and "schema"–the schema to which the data element belongs or the schema used to format the data element. Different discussions of metadata may refer to these attributes by different names, but the concepts behind the attributes remain the same. Each of these attributes is discussed in turn.

"Type" is used to add qualifications, or additional definition, to data elements, such as the qualifiers "medium" and "extent" to the data element "format" in Dublin Core. Type can be used as an attribute for a data element or, depending on the specificity of an application profile or schema, type can create a new data element from a broader data element. So why have a type attribute at all? Why not just acknowledge that the data element was too broad in the first place? The reason is that the metadata architecture needs to be flexible and extensible to support a variety of purposes. The root metadata schema must accurately describe an information object and support initial discovery and basic evaluation of the information object by the end user. However, it must also flexibly map to other standards, which may be more specific than one's root schema.

For example, if Dublin Core is the root schema, a data element may be "creator," which is a broadly shareable data element for data sharing initiatives such as Open Archives Initiative or Z39.50. It conveys adequate semantic meaning to an end user to enable the end user to discover and evaluate an information object. It maps readily to other standards, such as MARC, but not at an identical granular, or one-to-one mapping, level. A gross mapping may meet one's needs initially, but as collection needs change, a finer, more granular mapping may be needed. For example, the Georgia Tech Library is beginning two digital text projects–sponsored research reports and digital theses and dissertations. Both of these collections have been cataloged for years in their analog formats in the library's MARC-based catalog. However, in their digital form, they will be cataloged in Dublin Core for searching and retrieval via digital text portals.

To insure equal accessibility between the large amount analog, shelved materials and the smaller, full-text digital collections, two strategies will be employed: federated searching across the MARC catalog and offering the Dublin Core database at the portal. The Dublin Core records will be exported in MARC format and loaded directly into the MARC database. Obviously, the more granular the mapping, the more meaningful the mapped record will be and the less editing will be required for the exported record. The goal is to transport the record from one database to another with no loss of meaning and with minimal or no editing required for the more complex and granular MARC record. By including the type attribute of "PersName," "CorpName," and "ConfName" for creator and contributor, the data elements can map more readily to separate MARC elements of 100/700, 110/710 and 111/711. At the same time, this level of granularity may not be required for discovery and access within the root schema, and therefore do not require, for the Georgia Tech Community, separate data elements–a reminder that the primary user base drives the decision-making for the metadata schema.

When determining whether to create a separate data element, such as the MARC decision to have separate data elements for persons, corporations or conferences, it is necessary to step back and take a broad view of the applications and uses the metadata system will serve. If data sharing within a larger community is important, then less granular data elements ("creator," "contributor," etc.) should be used, with the attribute "type" used to provide semantic granularity when needed for mapping or for specific collections or applications where granularity is needed. Georgia Tech's sponsored research collection always includes a "sponsor" field, for the entity providing the grant funds. "Sponsor" is almost exclusively a corporate entity, so the "type" attribute could be used to derive a browseable corporate name index by the search engine.

"Role" is an important but neglected attribute for "agent" data elements. Agent data elements can be broadly defined, in modeling terms, as those entities that act upon or have responsibility for the information object in some way. Examples of agents in Dublin Core include creator, contributor and publisher. Within these data elements, different roles, such as "author," "editor," "distributor," "interviewer," "producer," etc., are performed. Roles are particularly critical for information objects in audiovisual formats, such as moving images or audio formats. Think, for example, of the many roles played by creators (those with primary responsibility for the intellectual content of an information object) and contributors (those with secondary or contributory responsibility) in the creation of a feature film. The creator may be the producer or the director (depending on the decision of the information community), while the contributors can include the screenwriter, the cinematographer, the music composer, the principal actors, the film editors, and, as appropriate, the author of the book from which the feature film is derived (for example, Margaret Mitchell, the author on whose book the MGM classic *Gone with the Wind* is based). For footage licensing purposes, the distributor or the rights holder (both of which are possible roles for the data element "publisher") is as critical for licensing and royalty distribution as the original publisher.

The Georgia Tech Library uses roles to great effect to customize search, display and entry screens for different communities within the Georgia Tech information universe. For example, to build the forthcoming digital theses and dissertations collection, students will accompany their theses and dissertations with simple forms including basic Dublin Core elements of creator, contributor, and publisher. However, these agent elements will be labeled by role: creator; thesis advisor; committee member; and department. Search screens and displays will reflect these roles, which are more meaningful to the user community than the data elements. However, when the metadata records are shared with the Networked Library of Digital Theses and Dissertations (NLDTD) in the required Dublin Core format, the data elements will be exported without roles for maximum interoperability within a large, international consortium. As this example, and the examples for "type" demonstrate, attributes can be used with great effect to add extensibility, flexibility and personalization to a metadata schema, without sacrificing interoperability and future extensibility, as user needs and metadata schemas evolve.

"Label" is used to separate semantic meaning from the basic display label for a metadata schema. At Rutgers University, librarians are developing a format-independent core metadata schema that will use "label" to distinguish data element use among a limitless number of metadata schema. Rutgers is evolving a metadata core that will be used to map among any metadata schema in use among the various libraries and departments engaged in digital activities at the many Rutgers University Libraries. For records expressed in the Rutgers core format, the data element name and the label will be the same. However, the records will be expressed in multiple formats by varying the schema and the label attributes. These attributes will be programmatically enabled to allow end users and metadata developers to move quickly and easily among metadata schemas for customized indexing, search, and display while the core format serves as a unifying element among all the digital projects in the Rutgers digital library environment. The Association of Moving Image Archivists (AMIA) are developing a union catalog–the AMIA Moving Image Gateway, with a core or root metadata standard to which all incoming records will be mapped. Schema and label attributes will be used to provide searchability, export, and display in any format supported by the Gateway, as well as to support custom display and export for each participating archive. Dynamic Web pages and search screens will allow each archive to have a Web presence personalized to their collection. An additional attribute, record location, will support record display in the data element order of the home database for transparent access to information, whether retrieved via the Gateway or using the archive's in-house metadata system.

The final attribute to consider is "schema." Schema is both an attribute of the data element and an attribute of the data value, discussed later. Schema is used to differentiate among labels to support multiple schemas in an extensible record and to indicate controlled vocabularies or formatting principles for data elements and data element attributes, such as roles, which may use controlled vocabularies such as the Getty *Art & Architecture Thesaurus*. The schema attribute has its own attributes or qualifiers, such as version number or online registry identifier (Uniform Resource Number or Uniform Resource Locator).

The final component of a metadata record is the "data value," the information specific to the described object that populates each data element in a metadata record for that object. For example, the creator (data element) of this paper is Grace Agnew (data value). Data values should be formulated according to a controlled vocabulary (such as the *Library of Congress Subject Headings*) or according to a formatting principle, such as the *Anglo-American Cataloguing Rules*, 2nd ed. (AACR2), which dictates that the above data value is expressed in inverted last name, first name format (Agnew, Grace). Data values should include a schema attribute, which indicates how the value is formulated. Again, the schema attribute itself will have attributes for version number and the online registry for the schema. This will enable future machine processing by search engines designed to reference and utilize online registries.

APPLICATION PROFILE

Once one has determined the data elements to be used, the attributes of those data elements, the order in which the data elements will display in the primary record display format, and whether each element is repeatable, mandatory, or optional, it is time to document the application profile. Documentation should occur in an online registry format according to International Standards Organization (ISO) standard 11179. ISO 11179 emerged primarily from the federal government data management environment. The primary goals of a registry formulated according to ISO 11179 are to standardize representation of the data element to enable shareability and durability (reuse) of the data element and the data values that populate the data element and to establish context and meaning for intelligent retrieval and interpretation of data. ISO 11179 consists of six parts:

- 11179-1 Framework for the Specification and Standardization of Data Elements
- 11179-2 Classification for Data Elements
- 11179-3 Basic Attributes of Data Elements
- 11179-4 Rules and Guidelines for the Formulation of Data Definitions
- 11179-5 Naming and Identification Principles for Data Elements
- 11179-6 Registration of Data Elements.

ISO 11179, which is available from the National Information Standards Organization (NISO), in Washington, D.C., is currently in a state of flux as the standard is rewritten to support model-based principles. In particular, 11179-3 is being completely rewritten in a data model format. The entire standard supports not just the identification and description of data elements but the entire registration process, including the establishment of the metadata creators as an identified registration authority. A registry can be expressed in many formats. The Video Development Group (ViDe) is currently developing a registry for its application profile of Dublin Core for digital video in XML/RDF (Resource Description Framework).

In an ISO 11179-compliant registry, each data element would receive a unique, unintelligent number to create a reusable, language-independent, machine-interpretable, data element. Other elements include the data element, name, the data element label, the definition, and the value domain (the contextual framework) within which the values reside. For example, "U.S. state" is a location that can be used in a mail delivery context or a subject access context. Within each value domain, different formatting principles would apply (for example, the use of official state abbreviations as a controlled vocabulary for mail delivery versus the state name spelled out as a controlled vocabulary subject heading). At a minimum, an ISO 11179-compliant registry should have the following twelve elements:

- Unique numeric identifier (for reusability)
- Data element name
- Data element label
- Data element version (numeric or date or both)
- Data element definition

- Data element obligation (mandatory, optional, recommended)
- Data element repeatability
- Value domain name
- Value domain definition
- Registration authority (Valid RA Code developed according to ISO 11179 and registered)
- Registration status (recorded, certified, standard)
- Administration status (in quality review, no further action, final).

The final two elements–registration status and administration status–refer to the status of the data element registration within the registry. Elements begin as proposals for evaluation and comment by the user community. Only after evaluation and revision by the community would a data element registration move from status of "recorded" and an administration status of "in quality review" to a final, standardized element available for full reusability by an international community. Obviously, a registry is going to use the identifier, definition, labels, etc., of the creator or managing authority (such as the Dublin Core Metadata Initiative, for Dublin Core). When creating a registry, information is given for those elements that have been added or customized for a particular application profile.

In addition to descriptive metadata elements, a metadata record may include administrative or meta-metadata elements. Examples include the metadata creator, date of creation, date of modification, and date of deletion. This last element is very important because most metadata is stored in a database management system, many of which make no provision for storing and maintaining deleted records. Populating a "date of deletion" data element with a date value can be used to trigger the writing of a brief record to a deleted record database, or a table that can track record deletions away from the live database. This can be critical for supporting union catalog initiatives where records are sent to a host site automatically based on modification date. For the union catalog to be accurate, deleted records must also be identified and transmitted. Another critical administrative data element is the "Archive identifier." A database can support multiple archive identifiers for independent contributors to the database, such as a consortial database with many participating institutions, for example, the AMIA Moving Image Gateway.

Once the schemas and an application profile for each schema are established, one must decide how to create and store the metadata records. Two currently valid options include relational database management systems (or alternatively, object-relational database management systems) or online storage in a Web-enabled storage and display format such as HTML or

XML. HTML metadata can be stored directly within <meta> tags in the header of an HTML page. Systems currently exist that will "scrape" this metadata from a contributing page to populate a fielded relational database, thus providing both intrinsic and extrinsic metadata. A better alternative is to provide metadata in XML (eXtensible Markup Language). (XML is currently well-known enough in the library community that a discussion of the benefits of XML over HTML is not necessary.)

XML metadata can be provided in the header and scraped, as described above, or stored in a relational database and staged for export and display in XML formats (which are dynamically repurposed as HTML displays using a style sheet, either Cascading Style Sheets or XML Style Sheet Language Transformations). Newer versions of relational database management systems, such as Oracle v. 9, IBM's DB2 and the open source Zope DBMS, now support or will soon support storage of tagged XML elements. Native XML databases are also available but are currently not recommended since the tools to index them, share the data, and repurpose the record display in response to queries are not readily available or mature. At this writing, native XML databases are a bleeding edge technology that should be studied and tested rather than actively utilized.

To utilize XML effectively as a display, storage, or transport format, it is necessary to document the metadata record as an XML object through the use of a document type definition or schema. Document type definitions define how a conformant metadata record will be constructed and displayed, and allow for validation against the specifications to insure conformance using primarily elements, attributes, and entities. XML schemas, which are slowly replacing document type definitions, use these same concepts but add modeling characteristics, object characteristics (such as attribute inheritance from a higher level element) and modularity to construct a schema that can be, in theory, combined with other schema in a modular fashion to create a "metaschema," and that provides a more object-oriented, less textual approach to XML object creation and validation. Tools for creating and validating schema are not as widespread as document type definition tools. I recommend, if one is new to XML, that he or she begin by creating and validating a document type definition and, then, migrate that to an XML schema.

CONCLUSION

Although the benefits of XML are largely familiar, I want to close with a discussion of what may be its most important benefit–that of data transport and sharing. I have alluded several times to the Open Archives Initiative protocol (OAI). OAI is a simple, HTTP-based protocol that mines records automatically from participating metadata repositories to create union catalogs or virtual exhibits. OAI retrieves records according to certain constraints: archive ID, datestamp (date created, date modified and date deleted), and set ID (corresponding roughly to collection or subject, as defined by the participants in the collaboration). OAI requires that Dublin Core simple (unqualified) in XML be supported as a base common denominator metadata record standard. XML, as a very flexible, customizable data storage and display standard, is ideal for transport of data within and among information communities.

The Resource Description Framework (RDF), alluded to earlier, is an XML-based wrapper for transporting data elements that can reference metadata registries using the XML namespace for the machine-processing of data elements from distributed metadata registries. Another standard to watch is the XML-based Simple Object Access Protocol (SOAP), a data transport standard that transports the data payload in an XML format together with headers that can include programmed addressing or processing instructions that are stripped off before the payload is delivered to the end user. Increasingly, XML will also enable automatic metadata generation as XML-created data objects populate the Web and are available to be mined for specific elements, which are scraped and written to metadatabases.

This is a necessarily brief look at the development of a flexible, extensible metadata system. One principle to take away from this paper is that "less is more." Developing a "core" or root metadata scheme is deceptively simple but will form the foundation of an extensible metadata architecture to enable end users to personalize their discovery and access to the evolving, expanding universe of digital information.

STANDARDS REFERENCED IN THIS PAPER

Anglo-American Cataloguing Rules, available at http://www.nlc-bnc.ca/jsc/.
CIDOC–Museum Information Reference Model, available at http://www.cidoc.icom.org/.
CSGDM (Content Standard for Digital Geospatial Metadata, more commonly known as "FDGC"), available at http://www.fgdc.gov/publications/documents/di.
CSS (Cascading Style Sheets), available at http://www.w3.org/Style/CSS/.
Dublin Core, available at http://www.dublincore.org.
EAD (Encoded Archival Description), available at http://www.loc.gov/ead/.
HTML (Hypertext Markup Language), available at http://www.w3.org/MarkUp/.

ISBD (International Standard Bibliographic Description), available at http://www.ifla.org/ VI/3/nd1/isbdlist.htm.

MARC (MAchine Readable Cataloging), available at http://www.loc.gov/marc/.

ISO 11179, available at http://xw2k.sdct.itl.nist.gov/l8/document-library/projects/ 11179-Revision/.

MPEG-7 (Motion Picture Experts Group), available at http://mpeg.telecomitalialab.com/ standards/mpeg-7/mpeg-7.htm.

Open Archives Initiative (OAI) Protocol, available at http://www.openarchives.org/.

Program for Cooperative Cataloging (PCC) MARC Core Record, available at http://lcweb.loc.gov/catdir/pcc/pcc.html.

RDF (Resource Description Framework), available at http://www.w3.org/RDF/.

SOAP (Simple Object Access Protocol), available at http://www.w3.org/TR/SOAP/.

TEI (Text Encoding Initiative), available at http://www.tei-c.org/.

XML (Extensible Markup Language), available at http://www.w3.org/XML/.

XSLT (XML Style Sheet Language Transformations), available at http://www.w3.org/ TR/xslt.

AUTHOR NOTE

Grace Agnew is currently Associate University Librarian for Digital Library Systems at Rutgers, the State University of New Jersey. She is the chair of the ViDe Video Access Working Group, which recently issued an application profile for using Dublin Core to describe digital video. She chaired the program committee for the August 2001 Managing Digital Video Content workshop, co-sponsored by ViDe, CNI, Internet2, and SURA. She is also a member of the I2 Middleware for Video (VidMid) working group.

Ms. Agnew is also a faculty member in the ALA ALCTS AACR2 Metadata Institute and an instructor at the Southeastern Library Network Digital Imaging Workshop. She is a consultant for the Association of Moving Image Archivists (AMIA) for the design of the AMIA Moving Image Gateway, a union catalog of moving image archives worldwide.

She is the author of numerous presentations, white papers, and articles on metadata and digital video, and co-authored the book, *Getting Mileage Out of Metadata*, published by the Library & Information Technology Association (LITA) of the American Library Association.

Practical Issues
in Applying Metadata Schemas
and Controlled Vocabularies
to Cultural Heritage Information

Murtha Baca

SUMMARY. Gives an overview of descriptive metadata schemas for art and architecture, including Categories for the Description of Works of Art, Object ID, and the VRA Core Categories. It also focuses on the menu of controlled vocabularies and classification systems needed to populate these metadata schemas, such as the *Art & Architecture Thesaurus, ICONCLASS*, and others. Addresses the development of local authority files and thesauri to enhance end-user access, and metadata mapping and crosswalks as a means of providing integrated access to diverse information resources. *[Article copies available for a fee from The Haworth Document Delivery Service: 1-800-HAWORTH. E-mail address: <docdelivery@haworthpress. com> Website: <http://www.HaworthPress.com> © 2003 by The Haworth Press, Inc. All rights reserved.]*

KEYWORDS. Art, architecture, metadata standards, controlled vocabularies, classification systems, metadata crosswalks

INTRODUCTION

In a paper presented at the ALCTS Metadata Preconference in Chicago in 2000, the author gave an overview and brief history of metadata stan-

Murtha Baca is Head, Standards Program, Getty Research Institute, 1200 Getty Center Drive, Suite 1100, Los Angeles, CA 90049-1688 (E-mail: mbaca@getty.edu).

[Haworth co-indexing entry note]: "Practical Issues in Applying Metadata Schemas and Controlled Vocabularies to Cultural Heritage Information." Baca, Murtha. Co-published simultaneously in *Cataloging & Classification Quarterly* (The Haworth Information Press, an imprint of The Haworth Press, Inc.) Vol. 36, No. 3/4, 2003, pp. 47-55; and: *Electronic Cataloging: AACR2 and Metadata for Serials and Monographs* (ed: Sheila S. Intner, Sally C. Tseng, and Mary Lynette Larsgaard) The Haworth Information Press, an imprint of The Haworth Press, Inc., 2003, pp. 47-55. Single or multiple copies of this article are available for a fee from The Haworth Document Delivery Service [1-800- HAWORTH, 9:00 a.m. - 5:00 p.m. (EST). E-mail address: docdelivery@haworthpress.com].

10.1300/J104v36n03_05

dards and controlled vocabularies for art, architecture, and material culture information.[1] In this paper, the author focuses on the selection of appropriate metadata schemas for cultural heritage resources; the role of metadata mapping and "crosswalks"; and the use of structured vocabularies and thesauri for populating metadata schemas to increase both precision and recall in end-user retrieval. The examples come from the realm of art and cultural heritage information, but the principles and types of tools discussed here can apply to metadata and controlled vocabularies in any area of study.

SELECTING METADATA SCHEMAS

Something that people whose task is to build information resources tend to forget or ignore is that there is no "one-size-fits-all" metadata scheme. There are good reasons why different metadata schemes have been developed over the years: MARC (MAchine Readable Cataloging) for bibliographic items, EAD (Encoding for Archival Data) for intact archival collections with a common provenance, CDWA (Categories for the Description of Works of Art) for art objects, VRA Core (Visual Resources Association Core) for visual surrogates of works of art and architecture, and Dublin Core for Web resources, which also serves as a "lowest common denominator" for mapping diverse information resources.[2] MARC even has different "flavors" for visual materials, archival materials and manuscripts, sound recordings, electronic resources, and other types of media. Selecting an inappropriate metadata scheme for a particular type of information resource or collection of materials can do a considerable disservice to both the materials themselves and to their intended end-users. Dublin Core, for example, was not conceived as a metadata scheme for cataloging art objects[3] and EAD was not developed as a "container" into which diverse art museum objects, all with a different provenance and no hierarchical relationship among them, should be forced.[4] Therefore, the first crucial step in creating effective art or cultural heritage information resources is to select the appropriate metadata schema (or subset, or adaptation thereof) for the materials to be described.

If the focus is on the art object itself, from a researcher's or even a non-expert user's point of view, the most appropriate schema to apply may be a subset of CDWA.[5] The data dictionaries of some major museum collection management systems, in fact, are based on and/or map to CDWA.[6] The Art Museum Image Consortium (AMICO) data dictionary is based on CDWA.[7] The national documentation system for all

Chilean state museums, "SUR," is based directly on CDWA. A Chinese-language version is currently being developed by the Academia Sinica in Taiwan.[8] If, instead, the focus is on managing and providing access to visual surrogates (such as photographs, slides, and digital images) of works of art and architecture, the VRA Core Categories may be the most appropriate metadata schema to use. Object ID is a simple metadata schema for describing and tracking art objects and antiquities as property, and does not focus on historical or contextual information. Such information may be of interest to scholars and researchers, but would not be important, for example, to a customs inspector or Interpol agent whose focus is identifying and possibly recovering a particular work.[9] Dublin Core is a relatively simple set of metadata elements designed to facilitate resource discovery online, and as a mapping tool to reconcile different metadata elements, but it does not provide sufficient information for other purposes.

METADATA MAPPING AND CROSSWALKS

As already mentioned, specific metadata schemas and element sets are the result of a long process of in-depth analysis and consensus building by members of the communities involved. Therefore, the first step in building an information resource or federating resources from a variety of departments within an institution or among different institutions is to select the metadata "container" most appropriate for the particular material. But, one might ask, if that is done, what happens to the idea of cross-resource searching of and access to resources encoded according to diverse metadata schemas? If we do not encode diverse resources according to the same schema, how can we provide integrated access to them? The answer is a combination of technological solutions (for example, information protocols like Z39.50 and markup languages like XML) and metadata mapping.

Metadata mapping is the process of identifying equivalent or nearly equivalent metadata elements or groups of metadata elements within different metadata schemas, carried out in order to facilitate semantic interoperability. Semantic interoperability is the ability to search seamlessly for digital information across heterogeneous distributed databases as if they were all part of the same virtual repository. This is the kind of integrated access we all dream about and promise both our institutional leaders and our end-users we will be able to deliver someday. The process of identifying the correspondences (and non-correspondences) between different metadata element sets produces a "crosswalk," which is a chart or table that represents the semantic mapping of fields or data elements in one element set to fields or data elements in another element set. (See Figure 1 for a sample mapping of the metadata elements in Categories for the Description of Works of Art, the VRA Core Categories, Encoded Archival Description, and the Dublin Core metadata element set.)

In addition to making it possible for heterogeneous information resources to be searched simultaneously with a single query as if they were all in the same repository, crosswalks can also make it possible to convert data effectively from one metadata standard to another, for example, to generate Dublin Core records from pre-existing MARC records. A crosswalk containing the fifteen Dublin Core elements (or a subset thereof) as a "switching language" can facilitate the process of creating an integrated search function. It is important to stress, however, that the process of metadata mapping is not a simple one, and must be carried out by persons who are well-versed in the metadata element sets and information resources involved. Machine mapping or less-than-precise mapping by people who do not understand the various metadata element sets can turn out to be totally ineffectual. For example: if mapping were being done to enable integrated access to MARC records for bibliographic materials in an art library

FIGURE 1. Sample Mapping of Metadata Schemas for Museum, Bibliographic, Archival, and Web Resources

CDWA	MARC	EAD	Dublin Core
Object/Work-Type	655 Genre-form	<controlaccess><genreform>	Type
Titles or Names	24Xa Title and Title-Related Information	<unittitle>	Title
Creation – Date	260c Imprint-Date of Publication	<unitdate>	Date.Created
Creation-Creator-Identity	1XX Main Entry 7XX Added Entry	<origination><persname> <origination><corpname> <origination><famname> <controlaccess><persname> <controlaccess><corpname>	Creator
Subject Matter	520 Summary, etc. 6xx Subject Headings	 <scopecontent> <controlaccess><subject>	Subject
Current Location	852 Location	<repository><physloc>	

and records formulated according to CDWA or the VRA Core Categories for art objects, how should the "creator" category in CDWA or VRA map to MARC in a meaningful way? If the end-user is going to be presented with a search box to search for "artist" or "creator," which fields in the underlying repositories should be queried? Obviously, for CDWA and VRA, the fields corresponding to "Creator-Name" (CDWA) and "Creator.Personal name" (VRA) will be searched. But what field(s) should be searched in the MARC records? The 100, 400, and 700 fields in MARC are for the creator or author, but in most cases this will be the author of a book, not an artist or creator of a work of art. "Creator" in the sense of an artist might more plausibly be found in the MARC 600 fields, which are for subject headings, or even in the 520 (Summary) field. Thus, if an end-user searched on Picasso or Pinturicchio in the "creator" field of a virtual repository, the search engine should look at the "Creator-Name" field in CDWA records, the "Creator.Personal name" field in VRA records, and the 700 and 520 fields in MARC records in order to retrieve meaningful results.

The foregoing example demonstrates why the intellectual process of metadata mapping must be done by knowledgeable human beings familiar with both the intellectual content of the particular information resources and the various metadata schemas being mapped. Only after that has been done can the actual data conversion process occur or cross-repository searching be carried out by a computer program. In addition, the decisions as to how the results of such integrated searches will be displayed must be the result of careful analysis of the records themselves, and end-user studies carried out *before* the data are made available publicly on the Web. Sorting and displaying search results by resource type–bibliographic record, EAD finding aid, museum object record, photograph record, or digital image record–might be one way to help end-users understand what they retrieve from a cross-repository search. Relevance ranking also should be considered. As it currently exists in most information systems, relevance ranking is unreliable at best and useless at worst. In larger and more diverse databases, ranking might be expected to assume greater importance to searchers, saving time and effort in the evaluation of larger sets of retrieved information.

SUBJECT VOCABULARIES, THESAURI, AND CLASSIFICATIONS

Choosing the most appropriate metadata standard or standards for describing particular collections or materials is only the first step in building an effective, usable information resource. Unless the metadata elements or data structure are populated with the appropriate data values (terminology), the resource will be ineffectual and users will not be able to find what they are looking for, even if it is actually there. Again, there is no one-stop-shopping for the appropriate vocabulary tool for any given project. Rather, builders of information resources should select from the menu of vocabularies most appropriate for describing and providing access points to their particular collections. These might include, but are not limited to, tools such as *Library of Congress Subject Headings, Library of Congress Name Authority File, Art & Architecture Thesaurus, Union List of Artist Names, Thesaurus of Geographic Names, Thesaurus for Graphic Materials,* and *ICONCLASS* for art, architecture, and material culture.

Increasingly, institutions and projects, especially collaborative initiatives in a particular subject area, are finding that the most effective thing they can do to serve both their internal and external users is to build their own thesauri and classification systems, using terms from established, broadly accepted subject vocabularies like *Library of Congress Subject Headings* or the *Art & Architecture Thesaurus*, but also adding both preferred and variant terms from the specific field of study, and from sources both printed and human, both expert and non-expert.[10] Some leading museum collection management systems include built-in subject vocabularies and thesaurus building-tools to facilitate this process.[11]

BENEFITS TO END-USERS

Why is the use of subject vocabularies and thesauri so important for end-user access? Because users often have an idea in mind of what they are looking for, but do not know exactly what it is called. Objects, artists, places, concepts, etc., can be called by more than one name, and names may change depending upon the time and place in which they are being used. Modern-day Paris was known as Lutetia Parisiorum in Roman times. Florence, Italy is called Firenze in Italian, Florencia in Spanish, Florenz in German, and so on. The sixteenth-century Danish painter Bernhard Keil was known in Italy as *Monsù Bernardo* during the years he worked in that country. [Editor's note: The Library of Congress Name Authority record gives "Keil, Bernardo" as the authorized heading.] Examples abound. In addition, structured subject vocabularies and thesauri, which are constructed to explicitly show the relationships between and among concepts, provide powerful information for end-users in the form of broader and narrower terms. A searcher might want to find a specific type of French armchair and even picture what that object looks like, but have no idea what it is called. A thesaurus like the *Art & Architecture Thesaurus* "knows" that *bergères* and *fauteuils* are types of armchairs, so, if narrower terms of the broader term "chair" are used to assist the searcher, he or she will find records or Web pages with *bergères* and *fauteuils* even if the words "chair" or "armchair" do not explicitly appear. A geographical thesaurus like the TGN can retrieve records for all places in a particular province, county, or other political subdivision because it "knows" the names of all the narrower terms of that place. A structured vocabulary of artist information can alert end-users to related persons and entities that may be of interest; for example, in the *Union List of Artist Names*, the record for Andrea del Verrocchio is linked via the related term structure to the record for Leonardo da Vinci, who was Verrocchio's pupil and apprentice.

Following are a few real-life examples of how subject vocabularies can assist users in finding what they are searching for. A user searches on "Giambologna" in the collections of the Metropolitan Museum of Art on the Web[12] and retrieves no results. He happens to know that Giovanni da Bologna is another name form for this artist, but that search also retrieves no results. The only way works by this artist can be retrieved from the museum's Web site is by searching on the name form Giovanni Bologna, because it is the only name form associated with this artist in its system. If a controlled vocabulary or authority list of artists' names is used, the user should be able to search on any of the variations or alternate spellings of an artist's name and still retrieve relevant records, even if the particular variant used in the search does not occur in those records or in the Web pages being searched. Use of a structured vocabulary that clusters variant names and terms greatly enhances recall, because the user goes from getting no results to getting results matching all of the variant forms submitted to the search engine.

End-users of such "expert systems" are not limited to novices or the general public. For museum collection management systems, the end-users include everyone in the institution who uses the information in the database, from curatorial staff to registrars to the people in the museum digital imaging laboratory who need to keep digital surrogates linked to the record for the object that they depict. For example, in the Getty Museum's collections information system, a user in the education department can search on the term "andirons" and retrieve records for "firedogs," which is the term preferred by the curators in the department of decorative arts. The person could have also searched on the alternate spellings "fire-dogs" and "fire dogs," or on the broader guide term "fireplace equipment," because all of this information is stored in the system's thesaurus manager module.

CONCLUSION

Cultural heritage institutions are rushing to make their collections available online, but the decisions that must be made in order for online resources to be truly useful are often misunderstood. It is not enough to use some metadata standard. A metadata standard appropriate to the materials in hand and the intended end-users must be selected. Even the right choice of a metadata schema will not ensure good end-user access. To succeed, that schema must be populated with data values from a carefully selected menu of controlled subject vocabularies and classification systems. The dream of integrated access to diverse information resources is still just that–a dream. The dream can become a reality if those responsible for making cultural heritage information available online judiciously select and implement the appropriate metadata schemas, controlled subject vocabularies and thesauri, metadata crosswalks, and information technologies available to us today.

AUTHOR NOTE

Murtha Baca is Head of the Getty Standards and Vocabulary Programs, and oversees the creation of digital resources relating to the collections of the Getty Research Institute in Los Angeles. She has published extensively on data standards and controlled vocabularies for indexing and accessing cultural heritage information, especially with a view to providing end-user access to images and related data online. Dr. Baca has taught many workshops and seminars on metadata, visual resources cataloging, and thesaurus construction at museums, universities, and other organizations in North and South America and in Europe.

REFERENCES

1. "A Picture Is Worth a Thousand Words: Metadata for Art Objects and Their Visual Surrogates," In Wayne Jones et al., eds., *Cataloging the Web: Metadata, AACR, and MARC21* (Lanham, MD: Scarecrow Press, 2001), p. 131-138.

2. See http://lcweb.loc.gov/marc; http://lcweb.loc.gov/ead; http://www.getty.edu/research/institute/standards/cdwa; http://www.vraweb.org; and http://dublincore.org/documents/dces.

3. The CIMI Dublin Core testbed, though not intended to do so, clearly demonstrated that Dublin Core is not an appropriate metadata schema for cataloging individual museum objects. See www.cimi.org.

4. The project variously referred to on its own Web pages as "Museums and the Online Archive of California" and "Museums in the Online Archive of California" (MOAC) is a stunning example of an inappropriate use of EAD. See http://www.bampfa.berkeley.edu/moac/.

5. Because CDWA was intentionally developed to cover as many of the elements necessary to describe art objects, it contains hundreds of metadata elements. Obviously, it would be impractical to use all of these in any given system.

6. E.g., Gallery Systems' The Museum System; see www.gallerysystems.com.

7. See www.amico.org/AMICOlibrary/dataDictionary.html.

8. See Lina Nagel, "Using Standards in the Documentation of Museum Collections: Categories for the Description of Works of Art, Object ID, and other Standardization Tools," in *Spectra* 26, 1 (Spring 1999), pp. 36-39. The English-language version of the Academia Sinica Web site can be found at www.sinica.edu.tw/index.html.

9. See www.object-id.com.

10. To give just one example of many, a "Thesaurus for Manuscript Studies" is currently being developed by a collaborative project led by the University of London Library. See www.palaeography.ac.uk/.

11. The Museum System incorporates LCSH, the AAT, the ULAN, and the TGN, as well as a thesaurus manager for building collection-specific thesauri. See note 6 above.

12. http://www.metmuseum.org/collections/search.asp.

Digital Resources and Metadata Applications in the Shanghai Library

Yuan-liang Ma
Wei Liu

SUMMARY. The Shanghai Digital Library (SDL) is a component of the China Digital Library Project. This paper introduces the framework, goals, and contents of the China Digital Library Project. The vision, mission, system architecture, digital resources, and related major technology of the SDL project are discussed. Also, the background of the Chinese metadata application and the metadata scheme of the SDL are described, and the features of metadata application in practical cases are analyzed. Finally, current issues of metadata application and their solutions are suggested. *[Article copies available for a fee from The Haworth Document Delivery Service: 1-800-HAWORTH. E-mail address: <docdelivery@haworthpress.com> Website: <http://www.HaworthPress.com> © 2003 by The Haworth Press, Inc. All rights reserved.]*

KEYWORDS. Shanghai Digital Library, China Digital Library Project, metadata schemas, China Academic Library & Information System, CALIS, China Book and Documentation Center of Science and Technology, China National Knowledge Infrastructure

Yuan-liang Ma is Director, Shanghai Library, 1555 Huai Hai Zhong Lu, Shanghai 200031, China (E-mail: mayuanliang <ylma@libnet.sh.cn>). Wei Liu is Head, Computer System & Network Center, Shanghai Library, 1555 Huai Hai Zhong Lu, Shanghai 200031, China (E-mail: liuwei <wl@libnet.sh.cn>).

[Haworth co-indexing entry note]: "Digital Resources and Metadata Applications in the Shanghai Library." Ma, Yuan-liang, and Wei Liu. Co-published simultaneously in *Cataloging & Classification Quarterly* (The Haworth Information Press, an imprint of The Haworth Press, Inc.) Vol. 36, No. 3/4, 2003, pp. 57-70; and: *Electronic Cataloging: AACR2 and Metadata for Serials and Monographs* (ed: Sheila S. Intner, Sally C. Tseng, and Mary Lynette Larsgaard) The Haworth Information Press, an imprint of The Haworth Press, Inc., 2003, pp. 57-70. Single or multiple copies of this article are available for a fee from The Haworth Document Delivery Service [1-800-HAWORTH, 9:00 a.m. - 5:00 p.m. (EST). E-mail address: docdelivery@haworthpress.com].

57

INTRODUCTION

As we enter the 21st century, we find ourselves in a "digital age." According to reports, the amount of information produced in the world each year is about 1-2 exabytes. This information exists mainly in the form of images, sound, and data, and text files are only 0.003% of the total amount. At the same time, more than 90% of the new information is created, exists, and is retrieved in digital format. As a result, libraries, which have traditionally dealt with the tasks of preserving and delivering textual materials such as books and serials, are facing a need to reform. Libraries need to establish digital libraries, collect digital resources, create and store them, and make use of them digitally.

Chinese libraries have a long way to go regarding the digital library. On the one hand, with the expansion of a global economy, China's libraries need to collect and organize digital resources so that they are accessible on the Internet. They need to make digital resources available to information users. On the other hand, China's digital resources are only 4% of the total number of Web pages on the Internet. Chinese culture has a long and illustrious history of more than 5,000 years and is a major part of the world's cultural heritage. It therefore behooves Chinese libraries to digitize the excellent works of the Chinese culture and make it possible for the world to share this rich cultural heritage.

Before discussing digital resources and their applications in the Shanghai Library, the following section gives a brief general introduction to the development of digital libraries in China.

DIGITAL LIBRARIES IN CHINA

Chinese libraries have been paying close attention to the development of digital libraries worldwide. The Shanghai Library has a special channel on its Website that contains articles, books, and conference information dealing with digital library research, tracing the achievements of digital library development both at home and abroad and providing information to colleagues and readers interested in this area.

In 1996, Chinese libraries began to be engaged in the establishment of digital libraries. Governments at various levels attached great importance to this development and encouraged libraries to draft plans for digital library development. Special funds were allocated to support digital library projects. Research and development for Chinese digital libraries consisted of three development systems. The first system, led by the State Cultural Ministry, involves establishing digital libraries within the National Library of China and other major public libraries. The second system, led by the State Educational Ministry, was concerned with conducting research and developing digital libraries in China's major academic libraries. The third system, led by the State Scientific and Technological Ministry, the Chinese Academy of Science, and other related Ministries and Committees of the government, is establishing digital libraries in their affiliated libraries and information research institutes. These three systems have different focuses in the development of their digital libraries, and are coordinated by the Chinese Digital Library Project Joint Meeting. This Joint Meeting was organized by the State Cultural Ministry, and 21 related ministries and committees participated in it.

Project for China's Experimental Digital Library, the Chinese Pilot Digital Library Project (CPDLP)

In May 1996, the National Library of China, together with the major public libraries in the country, including the Shanghai Library, Liaoning Library, Nanjing Library, Zhongshan Library (Guangdong Provincial Dr. Sun Yat-sen Library) and Shenzheng Library, submitted a proposal for China's Experimental Digital Library Project to the State Planning and Development Committee. The project was instituted in 1997, and designated one of the State's key science and technology projects. It was completed in May 2001.

The Project for China's Experimental Digital Library aims to establish an experimental digital library system with the collaboration, resource sharing, and unity of all participants. It operates in a distributed environment formed with standardized and multitype resources. It is hoped that it will provide a practical implementation technique that can be used for the development of all digital libraries in China. Besides keeping track of international standards related to digital library development, the project has made significant contributions in: (1) designing an overall structure for the system; (2) achieving a distributed system across China; (3) developing practical applications for future use; and (4) designing and accomplishing a user-friendly interface across the network and distributed data resources. The project also conducts several successful programs and projects in China, including digitization projects for Chinese rare books, doctoral dissertations, historical maps and pictures, Shenzhen Local documents, Min Guo (1911-1949) publications, Northeast China Pictures and documents, and documents on global digital libraries.

This is the first digital library project in China and the first attempt to provide solutions to issues inherent in developing digital libraries in the country. The project needs further improvement in order to be put into widespread use in development of those digital libraries. The solution has three aspects: the digital resources construction system, the storage and management system, and the services system.

China Digital Library Program

As a major achievement of the Project for China's Experimental Digital Library, in July 1998, the National Library of China brought forward a China Digital Library Program proposal, which was approved by China's government. The goals of the program are as follows:

1. To form groups of large-scale and high-quality digital repositories with a capacity of not less than 20TB;
2. To provide domestic and global services via a national backbone communications network;
3. To integrate unitary technologies into the international mainstream technologically;
4. To realize the union acquisition, cataloging and interlibrary loan of documents among libraries throughout China;
5. To develop intelligent digital library application systems with Chinese characteristics;
6. To foster highly qualified professionals to support the sustainable development of the China Digital Library Program.

According to these goals, the major tasks of the program involve the creation of digital repositories, the construction of software/hardware infrastructure, the development of application systems, the shaping of standards and specifications structures, and the training of professionals.

Under the program, the National Library of China, in collaboration with other institutions, has completed the following projects:

1. Application of SGML in the Library
2. Knowledge Network: Systematic Digital Library Engineering
3. Study of Groups of Digital Libraries in Beijing Zhongguancun Hi-Tech Park
4. China Digital Library Application System under High-Speed Information Network
5. China's Experimental Digital Library
6. Experimental Digital Library Environment and Demonstration System.

China Academic Library & Information System (CALIS) Project

Led by the State Educational Ministry, the China Academic Library & Information System was approved by the State Project and Development Committee and launched in November 1998.

The China Academic Library & Information System Project is a library-networking project, aimed at Web information resource sharing via the China Education and Research Network (CERNET) for faculties of colleges and universities, accommodating a continuous flow of information resources and development of telecommunication networks. With Web-based distribution technology, academic libraries are able to make full use of their large numbers of digital resources and speed up the development of their databases. The project uses methods employed by foreign libraries, integrates new achievements of technology, and features databases originated locally for its online cooperative cataloging system as well as a customized online public access catalog and interlibrary loan system.

The major content and task of the China Academic Library & Information System is:

1. *Construction of a documentation and information service network:* Establishing a tri-level network based on the China Education and Research Network consisting of national centers, regional centers, and academic libraries is the principal task the System was to accomplish. This network includes four national documentation and information centers on the subjects of arts and sciences, engineering, agriculture and medicine, seven regional documentation and information centers (Southeast China, North China, South China, Central China, Southwest China, Northwest China and Northeast China), and academic libraries participating in the system. There are mirror sites at each national and regional center.

2. *Documentation, information resources, and digital construction:* A union catalog of books and periodicals was built based on the holdings in each participating library. Seven regional union catalog databases were established, and a number of foreign information databases were purchased or leased, in order to be incorporated into a reference resource of larger dimensions. The project also included documentation for the holdings of several Chinese academic institutions and their information databases, a number of which were major discipline-specific databases.

3. *Services of the China Academic Library & Information System (CALIS):* Areas of service to be provided by the new CALIS system include public information access; interlibrary loan; document delivery;

electronic resources navigation; cooperative online cataloging; and cooperative acquisitions. Currently, CALIS offerings include the following:

- Union Database of Books and Periodicals, which provides information on the holdings of 100 academic libraries;
- Chinese Periodicals Current Contents Database, which contains information for tables of contents of more than 5,000 current Chinese periodicals;
- Thesis and Dissertation Database, which enables searching and retrieval of theses and dissertations from 61 universities across the nation; and,
- Conference Proceedings Database, which offers searching and retrieval of the proceedings of international conferences held within China.

The databases named above are augmented by eleven databases purchased or leased from external sources. They are Academic Search Elite; Business Source Elite; OCLC; Business Source Premier; China InfoBank; Ei Village; Genome Database; ProQuest Academic Research Library; Uncover Science Citation Index CSA; ProQuest Digital Dissertations; and Science Online Elsevier.

China Book and Documentation Center of Science and Technology

Led by the State Scientific and Technological Ministry and approved by the State Council, the China Book and Document Center of Science and Technology was established in June 2000. The center is actually a virtual scientific and technological information resource network. The participating institutions are the China Academy of Science Library, the China Scientific and Technological Information Research Institute, the Mechanical Industry Information Research Institute, the Metallurgical Industry Information and Standard Research Institute, the China Chemical Industry Information Center, the China Academy of Agriculture Library and the China Academy of Medicine Library. In all, there are seven libraries and institutes involved.

The goal of the development process is to create a national scientific and technological resource collection and service consortium. The general principle on which the consortium is based is that each institute will process data and provide services separately, but will cooperate in establishing a central database for uniform information retrieval. The center will provide users with secondary document retrieval services and primary document delivery services through the Internet. Any Internet users can have free access to the secondary document retrieval service provided by the center. Registered users can also request the center to deliver primary documents in various ways, such as by e-mail, fax, and the postal service. At present, the databases available are the Foreign Scientific and Technological Periodical Database, Foreign Conference Proceedings Database, Foreign Book Database, Chinese Conference Proceedings Database, and Chinese Theses and Dissertation Databases.

The online information service system provides information retrieval service 24 hours a day. A request for primary documents is processed within two days; and, if the request is marked for rush service, in one. The online service system of the center is at: http://www.nstl.gov.cn.

China National Knowledge Infrastructure Base

Launched in June 2000, the China National Knowledge Infrastructure (CNKI) consists of over 70 special databases, covering subject areas such as theoretical research, policy research, laws and regulations, work discussions, current news and affairs and other related information.

The CNKI is based on the China Periodical Network Full-text Database and the China Major Newspaper Full-text Database created by the Qinghua University. In the future, CNKI developers will also select and compile information from both Chinese and foreign databases such as the China Laws and Regulations Database, the China Trade Standards Database and the Chinese Yearbooks Database. The CNKI knowledge base provides online subscription services. The project maintains a central website (CNKI.net and http://www.chinajournal.net.cn) and also has 80 mirror sites countrywide.

DIGITAL RESOURCES IN THE SHANGHAI LIBRARY

The Shanghai Library is the first public library in China to begin the construction of a digital library. Upon the completion of a new building and its opening to the public in December 1996, the library began to consider digitizing many items from its treasured special collections as well as acquiring electronic resources regularly. The basic information infrastructure, newly established at a cost of about $1,000,000 (U.S.), was expected to provide a variety of public services.

As a traditional library, the Shanghai Library is large in scale. It is located in the center of the city and has an area space of more than 84,000 square meters. The library has a collection of more than 13,000,000 books and 3,800,000 other documents, among which are a large number of precious historical documents unique to China. The library also subscribes to numerous foreign serials and scientific research materials. Approximately 10,000 visitors come to the library every day.

Facing the challenge of the Internet and digital media, the Shanghai Library has formulated a plan for the development of a digital library. In addition to strengthening network construction, the library has begun to digitize its historical documents as part of a larger preservation process, and began re-engineering its internal workflow to facilitate this. After a few years' effort, the library anticipates being able to provide most of its services through the Internet, and online services will become the major method of delivery.

The Shanghai municipal government has given strong support to the Shanghai Library's plan. Special funds for the digital library project are allocated to the library in each year's budget. The Shanghai Digital Library Initiative was launched in 1997. By 1999, seven digitization projects were completed. They began to provide services to the public in 2000, after the application system integration and software development were completed. For the next two years the focus was to integrate purchased digital resources into the service system of the digital library.

The Shanghai Library Digital Resource Collections

At this writing, the Shanghai Digital Library is an online library that contains nine resource databases, with about 200 gigabytes of data, most of which are scanned image data. Functionally, these resource databases can be divided into two categories. The first function is to disseminate information and preserve China's cultural heritage. These resources include Shanghai Pictures, Shanghai Local Documents, Chinese Traditional Opera, Chinese Rare Books, and Min Guo Books. The second function is to provide scientific education for Shanghai residents. The resources in this category are scientific and technological conference proceedings, Chinese newspapers and periodicals, the Western Periodical Content Database, and Popular Science Video Clips (http://www.digilib.sh.cn).

Brief descriptions of the components of Shanghai Library's Digital Library are in order.

1. The Old Shanghai Pictures traces the development of Shanghai as a city. It presents the history of Shanghai in the last 100 years with about 10,000 pictures in a large structure of texts and images.

2. The Shanghai Local Documents Database contains three sections–Shanghai Yearbooks, New Shanghai Local Documents, and Local Documents Catalog. The Shanghai Yearbooks contain 114 titles and 227 volumes of yearbooks in various subject fields for Shanghai be-

tween 1914 and 1999. The New Shanghai Local Documents contains 115 titles and 141 volumes of books that reflect the great change in, and achievements of, Shanghai over a period of twenty years of reform.

3. The Chinese Traditional Opera Database is a garden of various kinds of Chinese traditional performing arts. It contains an introduction to fifteen types of traditional performances and operas, biographies of famous actors and actresses, and about 5,000 minutes of audio recordings. Many of the collected arias are more than half a century old.

4. The Chinese Rare Books Database contains the treasures of Chinese traditional culture. The Shanghai Library has a collection of 1.7 million volumes of ancient and rare documents, among which are more than 70,000 rare book titles. More than 3,000 of them are evaluated as cultural antiquities. These books are of very important historical research and artistic value. Until now, 3,223 titles and 1.3 million pages have been digitized and are available on the Library intranet for browsing, printing, and downloading. Nineteen titles from among these documents are on the Internet.

5. The Min Guo Books, published from 1911 to 1949, are another special collection of the Shanghai Library and are the most complete of all similar collections in China's libraries. There are about 90,000 titles and more than 330,000 volumes in this collection. Digital resources include more than 1,000 titles of the representative works and all of the scanned images. These materials are available on the Internet.

6. Proceedings of scientific and technological conferences held in China since 1958 have been collected on an ongoing basis. At present, the Digital Library also contains about 27,000 conference papers recorded since 1986.

7. The Chinese Newspapers and Periodical Index of the Shanghai Library was first published in the 1950s. The Chinese Newspapers and Periodicals Database based on the Index is the best and the most complete reference tool for research on the subjects of philosophy and social science. Currently this database compiles and adds about 16,000 articles every year.

8. The Western Periodical Database is based on purchased foreign periodical content data and has a self-designed retrieval system. This database collects more than 15,000 Western periodicals, covering almost all the foreign periodicals commonly used in China, and has multiple search fields. The Digital Library of the Shanghai Library provides additional services such as full-text photocopying, interlibrary loan and customized document delivery, etc.

9. The Popular Science Video Clips have collected 100 episodes of popular science serials "3 Minutes of New Science and Technology," and 41 episodes of "8 Minutes of Science and Wisdom." There are altogether over 700 minutes of video programs.

Collections of the Shanghai Digital Library*

Database Name	Materials on the Internet	Scale of the Database
Old Shanghai Pictures	10,000 old pictures	over 20,000 old pictures
Shanghai Local Documents	307 books	114 titles and 227 volumes of yearbooks, 115 titles and 141 volumes of books
Chinese Traditional Opera	15 kinds of traditional operas, 90 actors and actresses, 311 arias and about 5,000 minutes	Same with the left column
Chinese Rare Books	19 titles	about 1.3 million pages, 313 CD-ROMs, 3,223 titles
Min Guo Books	18 books	over 1,000 books in the form of scanned images
Chinese Newspapers and Periodicals	160,000 articles in the form of scanned images	Same with the left column
Proceedings Index	27,000 records of articles	Same with the left column
Western Periodical Database	Current contents	Same with the left column
Popular Science Video Clips	141 episodes of popular science serials	about 700 minutes of programs

*Figures quoted as of August 2001

The Structure and Features of the Shanghai Digital Library

Currently the Shanghai Digital Library system uses the IBM Digital Library (IBM Content Manager) as its major development tool. The system structure supports an object oriented and distributed resource organization model, which guarantees the flexibility and extensibility of the system when managing large amounts of different data resources. The content management adopts a metadata resource descriptive scheme based on the Dublin Core. This scheme uses XML/RDF as its framework and allows the coexistence of multiple metadata. It guarantees the integrity and interoperability of metadata in the content management of original materials. This entirely open structure has laid the foundation for the connection of digital libraries both at home (that is, in China) and abroad. Because of the application of JAVA and Servlet techniques, the whole system can run on both Windows and AIX platforms, and is able to have a mutual backup. It is reliable and has a low cost of operation. The search program of the system permits cross database index searching, full-text searching, or comprehensive searching that combines both index and full-text, and realizes the dynamic retrieval of resource content.

METADATA APPLICATION
IN THE SHANGHAI DIGITAL LIBRARY

In developing the Shanghai Digital Library, the metadata approach was the first thing to be considered in the design plan. It is the basis for digitizing document resources and is considered the key to building digital libraries with effective interoperability and extensibility. That is to say, the metadata approach is the core of a digital library. The following principles were considered in designing the metadata plan for the Shanghai Digital Library.

1. *Complexity of information resources:* The nature of the digital resources in the Shanghai Library is the first factor to consider. To be consistent with the goals of the Shanghai Digital Library, the metadata approach should be to develop electronic files of all kinds of information resources such as rare books, rubbings, genealogies, journal articles, patents, standards, and more. It should even aim to improve existing systems of databases, with full use of Chinese MARC (CNMARC). It should also provide a common foundation and an applied framework for resource description. Our metadata approach is to integrate several metadata plans–a fundamental requirement.

2. *Usability:* MARC is a valuable tool for libraries worldwide. It provides a complete description of content and form for information resources. It is capable of processing 99% of human recorded knowledge, but its costs are high for the large number of resources being processed in the Internet era. In addition, MARC cannot describe some special kinds of information resources. Therefore, it is essential to look for an easier, quicker, and less costly substitute. New methods of information processing should be used to meet new needs.

3. *Standardization:* The difficulty of achieving interoperability among metadata systems lies in the use of different standards that result in incompatible systems. Without interoperability, cross-database retrieval cannot be realized and the use of multiple databases is difficult. To choose among standards means to choose among technologies. Technical progress is ongoing and upgrading resources proves costly or even impossible for libraries lacking the funds. So, the choice among standards is of utmost importance. The concept of standards is relative; some *de facto* standards are actually more popular than national or international standards. Thus, close attention should be paid to the changing situation, and the most flexible and open standards should be adopted.

4. *Localization in Chinese characters and script:* Chinese resource descriptions have features different from those in roman scripts and,

therefore, need to be localized. This may appear to be a kind of customization, but the development of a digital library ultimately proves to be a form of globalization of Chinese resources, and should be able to reflect all the descriptive features. The metadata approach should be able to support universal applications, including those unique to Chinese resources. The issue of resource description localized in Chinese needs to be solved at the system level in order to support UNICODE. Resource descriptions need to support local elements, e.g., description of Chinese ancient books uses a special classification scheme–classics, history, philosophy and belles-lettres–the four traditional divisions of Chinese learning.

5. *Preservation aspects:* Along with museums, libraries house a great many items that are part of China's cultural heritage. Digitizing printed materials makes these treasures accessible by ordinary people while allowing the originals to be well preserved. The digital resources themselves face issues of perpetual preservation. With more and more publications created digitally, preservation of human intellectual resources is confronted with a new challenge. This needs to be considered while designing the metadata profile.

Based on the above principles, we investigated examples of digital libraries worldwide, observed and studied various metadata approaches, and eventually chose the metadata approach that applied Dublin Core as the core metadata element set, with other metadata methods describing the remainder of special resources. It is packaged in the XML/RDF model, and is the method of metadata application profile that Dublin Core recommends. This method enhances the ability to describe information resources using a standard metadata approach which promotes interoperability among metadata systems.

This approach using Dublin Core and other metadata methods gives consideration to various kinds of information resources. However, it is necessary to define the core metadata element set to ensure elementary interoperability between systems. It is applicable for describing general library resources, defined as document-like objects, in the Dublin Core metadata element set. This is the best way to meet the needs of digital libraries, and is widely accepted and applied throughout the world.

Such a standard, simple, syntax-clear core metadata element set makes it easier for conversion between and integration with a variety of metadata systems. In our approach, the core metadata element set serves as a bridge across various banks of resources. Other banks of resources use Dublin Core as the core metadata set or are dynamically converted into Dublin Core metadata to realize syntax interoperability between systems.

Dublin Core is easy to use and has become a universal standard. It provides for expansion through controlled Chinese characters and scripts. Many coding systems can be added, and XML/RDF supports SGML in Chinese, but a uniform standard is needed for cross-system use. Stronger interoperability between metadata systems is possible if a standard interface is adopted. Permanent preservation of information resources is possible with the International Standards Organization model of Open Archival Information System (OAIS), which strives to meet this authoritative requirement in management. Both humans and machines can understand Dublin Core metadata because it is independent of RDF syntax and uses SGML pure text. It can be easily inserted into various descriptive plans and is easy to upgrade, transport, and preserve.

CONCLUSION

Important steps forward are being taken with the fulfillment of these two new systems in the Shanghai Library. Nonetheless, they present challenges as well as opportunities.

The IBM Digital Library adopted in the applied system of the Shanghai Digital Library cannot process certain complex MARC data. As a result, when the system uploads metadata elements, we convert them into Dublin Core metadata elements. Such conversion creates many problems. First, non-symmetry between metadata system definitions leads to the loss of certain information or ambiguity of syntax during conversion. Second, some functions of the retrieval service are limited. In order to make up for the loss, we enter all the metadata resources in text format. They are loaded into the full-text search engine of the IBM Digital Library to provide efficient simple query service, including quasi-accurate full-text queries and fuzzy query functions. These functions raise the recall ratio for users and minimize the influence of syntactic ambiguity caused by metadata conversion in the system.

The online cooperative Chinese resource cataloging system offers a platform for online cataloging based on the Internet. The system supports cooperative cataloging and takes Chinese Web resources as its main objects of description. The system takes Dublin Core as its kernel and supports conversion of Chinese MARC and data input and output in formats of Chinese MARC, Dublin Core, RDF, XML, HTML, etc. The system also provides a series of automatic tools such as automatic Uniform Resource Locator (URL) verification and maintenance. It also facilitates prompt and efficient cataloging of online resources. In addition to that, the system includes functions of user management, fee management, retrieval service, and online training, which gives sound support to cooperative cataloging services.

In the process of designing the online cooperative Chinese resource cataloging system, we have consulted the OCLC Cooperative Online Resource Catalog program. We hope our system will succeed in becoming a large metadata application project similar to the Cooperative Online Resource Catalog program and will provide beneficial experience in applying and popularizing Chinese metadata systems within our country.

AUTHOR NOTES

Professor Yuan-liang Ma is the Director of the Shanghai Library (SL) and Institute of Scientific and Technical Information of Shanghai (ISTIS). He is Vice-President of the China Society for Library Sciences and Vice-President of the Society of Science & Technologic Information of China. Professor Ma received numerous awards for his achievements and contributions to Chinese library and information science and is a sought after speaker in China and abroad. He is a professor of the East China Normal University.

Wei Liu is the Head of the Computer System and Network Center of the Shanghai Library. He is responsible for the creation and development of the electronic and Web resources of the Library.

Struggling Toward Retrieval:
Alternatives
to Standard Operating Procedures
Can Help Librarians and the Public

Sheila S. Intner

SUMMARY. Starting points for cataloging and bibliographic control are assumptions that "the goal of libraries is to serve their patrons," and that documents should be identifiable individually as well as grouped with related items in an array from which patrons can choose what they wish. But, like all human endeavors, libraries and the world around them do not stand still. Ranganathan observed that "the library is a growing organism," which prompts us to consider change a fundamental value. Years later, Marshall McLuhan observed that "the medium is the message," highlighting the power and impact of physical form on the information it contained. Despite the author's strongly held belief in the value of standards and uniformity, which has made the exchange of computerized bibliographic data possible, she suggests libraries must move beyond accepting those values unconditionally to a new position in which customization assumes a higher priority. She looks to the world of commerce to explore potentially useful new approaches to cataloging and metadata. *[Article copies available for a fee from The Haworth Document Delivery Service: 1-800-HAWORTH. E-mail address: <docdelivery@haworthpress.com> Website: <http://www.HaworthPress.com> © 2003 by The Haworth Press, Inc. All rights reserved.]*

Sheila S. Intner is Professor and Founding Director, Simmons College GSLIS at Mount Holyoke College, Simmons College, 11 Hupi Woods Circle, P.O. Box 151, Monterey, MA 01245-0151 (E-mail: shemat@aol.com).

[Haworth co-indexing entry note]: "Struggling Toward Retrieval: Alternatives to Standard Operating Procedures Can Help Librarians and the Public." Intner, Sheila S. Co-published simultaneously in *Cataloging & Classification Quarterly* (The Haworth Information Press, an imprint of The Haworth Press, Inc.) Vol. 36, No. 3/4, 2003, pp. 71-86; and: *Electronic Cataloging: AACR2 and Metadata for Serials and Monographs* (ed: Sheila S. Intner, Sally C. Tseng, and Mary Lynette Larsgaard) The Haworth Information Press, an imprint of The Haworth Press, Inc., 2003, pp. 71-86. Single or multiple copies of this article are available for a fee from The Haworth Document Delivery Service [1-800- HAWORTH, 9:00 a.m. - 5:00 p.m. (EST). E-mail address: docdelivery@haworthpress.com].

http://www.haworthpress.com/store/product.asp?sku=J104
© 2003 by The Haworth Press, Inc. All rights reserved.
10.1300/J104v36n03_07

KEYWORDS. Cataloging standards, metadata, Cutter's objects, cataloging Websites

INTRODUCTION

Standardization versus customization has been debated for as long as I have been a librarian. Personally, I have always championed standardization, because it was a major factor in building the computerized bibliographic databases on which libraries relied to furnish access to larger and larger arrays of materials for their patrons. *Standard Cataloging for School and Public Libraries* is the name of my textbook, authored with Jean Weihs.[1] Developing standards for nonprint formats guided my involvement with the Audiovisual Committee of the Association for Library Collections & Technical Services, which I once chaired. Nevertheless, I agree that some audiences benefit from nonstandard practices designed to meet their particular needs; but, it takes more time, money, and effort to stray from standard operating practices, so one needs a compelling reason to do it. Something of great value should be gained in exchange for the added effort and cost–certainly something of more value to library patrons than the satisfaction of librarians doing what they wish.[2]

Being an educator rather than a practitioner, I have the luxury (one might say the obligation) of playing the devil's advocate about standards. My trust in them as the most effective way to maximize output and provide the greatest cataloging value to the library has never stopped me from questioning their efficacy. Knowing that I have this penchant, I was asked to speak about alternatives to standard cataloging operations for World Wide Web-based resources–an issue I believe becomes more important with each passing day as the balance of library collections shifts a little more toward electronic resources and away from traditional formats.[3] Before I do, however, allow me to review, briefly, what standards provide. Then, I shall explore how innovative practices might be applied to benefit library patrons who search for and use those materials.

ASSUMPTIONS AND ARGUMENTS

I believe two basic assumptions underlie current cataloging practice:

1. "the goal of libraries is to serve their patrons"[4]
2. Cutter's "Objects" embody the aims of cataloging, namely, that cataloging operations should produce data that identify individual items and collocate related items.[5]

Cutter thought in terms of authors, titles, and subjects as the main elements to be identified and collocated, but today we have added others such as dates, publishers, languages, etc., to his list of three. It seems fair to ask if these assumptions still hold in our present reality.

At the same time, two additional assumptions describe the environment in which libraries and their catalogs exist:

3. "the library is a growing organism"[6]
4. "the medium is the message."[7]

How do these last two assumptions impact the earlier ones governing cataloging practice? What arguments can be made in light of all these assumptions?

Assumptions 1 and 2 imply that patron needs, which should be the focus of our activities, are predictable and amenable to the application of standard methods. This may once have been true, when scholarship was rule-bound and disciplines had sharply-defined territory, but both appear to be quite fluid today, challenging our ability to make predictions that hold for most, if not all, patrons. Library patrons, once limited to an elite few, today include anyone on the planet with Internet access. Similarly, definitions of information needs, once limited in scope, genre, and format, are now anything one can envision–from the unedited footage of current or past events captured live on film or videotape, to complex global demographics obtained by census analyses, to configurations of buildings and other installations recorded by orbiting satellites–and the boundaries among disciplines are notoriously unclear.

Assumption 2 could be abbreviated as Find and Gather, or, in catalogers' terms, Describe and Collocate. But catalogs do more than that today, and, in addition, reflect a great deal of behind-the-scenes work that was taken for granted. Cutter's "Objects" assume someone previously selected the materials and acquired them for the library before catalogers worked on them. To be more accurate, we should expand Cutter's "Objects" to Select and Acquire, Describe and Collocate. Also, we might consider the outcome of these activities, which the library catalog facilitates. It can be expressed as Select Again and Use. The first selection assumes a librarian-selector starts with the entire universe of knowledge and culls from it that which best meets the needs of a local library, which will subsequently be acquired and cataloged for use onsite. The whole operation can be expressed as: (1) First Selection, (2) Acquisition, (3) Description, (4) Collocation, (5) Second Selection, and (6) Use.

Assumptions 3 and 4 describe aspects of change. Number 3, Ranganathan's Fifth Law of Librarianship, reminds us that because the environment in which we work undergoes constant change, it is natural to expect libraries and library practices to respond to those changes by evolving, also. Library practices respond to many kinds of change–in materials, in publication patterns, in delivery methods, in usage, and in media. The current environment–marked by high volume, diverse, changeable resources and a lack of unifying organizational principles for the Internet–can be expected to require the development of new and creative methods for reaching and serving the public.

The fourth assumption alerts us to potential change in three things: (1) electronic resources themselves; (2) cataloging displays; and (3) delivery of cataloging information to patrons via the Internet. The formats of both documents and catalogs have changed, which McLuhan points out affects their communicative powers. Much of what is being said at this Institute by other speakers is evidence we are responding to those changes. Moreover, patrons no longer have to go to a library to search its catalog. They can "let their fingers do the walking" and search electronically from any location, provided they can gain access.

Each of these changes has had a profound impact on library cataloging. The change from card catalogs to computer-based catalogs involved a leap that, at the time it began and for years afterward, we believed was a leap of giant proportions. Viewing it now, however, it may only be a small leap compared to the effects now rippling through our midst as a result of changing from bibliographic data functioning as surrogates separate from the documents they represent to embedded bibliographic data functioning as an integral part of the documents themselves. I believe that the nature of the relationship between metadata and electronic documents is a difference in kind, not a difference in extent. Cataloging needs to acknowledge this new relationship by incorporating new rules and practices into its functioning.

The Internet, with its vast number of information offerings, appears to possess a whole universe of knowledge. The key word here is "appears." Librarians know the Internet contains far from "everything," but it has enough material to look like a good imitation of "everything" to patrons. Academic librarians, in particular, complain that books and printed journals fail to compete successfully with electronic resources for students' attention, regardless of the actual value of the contents. Patrons simply telescope the six-stage operation involving numerous library specialists, support staff, and themselves into one giant step, and are lulled into thinking they can take that giant step alone with ease. If user-hostile systems requiring expert mediation were the hallmark of early mainframe-based computer systems, such as the original DIALOG system, user-friendliness requiring no knowledge at all is the hallmark of the Internet. Patrons are given tools to do the initial selection from the universe of electronic knowledge, dispense with the acquisition process, and skip the middle stage in which highly educated catalogers provided them with bibliographic systems and the need to make a second selection from a preselected population of high-quality items (often mediated for greater effectiveness by highly educated reference librarians). Instead, patrons now can move from first selection to use. By eliminating the library and the librarian's efforts from the scene, no expert in bibliographic organization, authentication, and selection works to ensure that the materials patrons find will be accurate or authoritative. Patrons find and gather materials–sometimes a considerable number of materials–but these materials have not been pre-selected, pre-organized and facilitated (read "cataloged") for retrieval.

HOW DOES STANDARD PRACTICE WORK?

Standard cataloging and classification practices require us to provide access via (1) principal creators, when their names are prominently displayed on the item being cataloged; (2) titles and title variations appearing on the item being cataloged; (3) series titles if items belong to series having titles of their own; (4) titles of individual works contained within a compilation, within reasonable limits; (5) subject words chosen from a controlled vocabulary to represent the contents of the item being cataloged; and (6) call numbers roughly representing the subject matter of the item being cataloged plus a shelf address where it is physically located. In addition, the programming of computerized catalogs enables us to provide access via keywords taken from titles, subjects, summaries, and other parts of cataloging records as well as enabling searchers to limit retrieval by date, language, and physical medium.

These are all valid access routes and no one doubts they should continue, despite the time it takes to prepare and implement them. As yet, no simpler, faster methods provide so much valuable information without sacrificing accuracy and precision. Some people think the current flood of electronic items will either bankrupt libraries that attempt to catalog them all thoroughly and comprehensively, or cause catalogers to throw up their hands in despair of ever managing it successfully. Others–this author included–are more optimistic and believe the task is daunting but possible. As some writers and speakers suggest, all that libraries should catalog are items selected for their collections, not everything, willy-nilly. And, of the items selected for cataloging, some might be treated less fully than others, as is now done for traditional materials.

Two aspects of cataloging practice–fullness and accuracy–will affect how well and how easily the flood of electronic resources can be managed. The Program for Cooperative Cataloging's (PCC) core record standards have shown that limited cataloging does not hamper access as much as no cataloging at all and, despite criticism, works well in practice. PCC records give basic identifying information only, but emphasize accuracy in selected access points over putting more effort into filling out the records. This strategy seems like a sensible adaptation for electronic resources. Accuracy, especially in retrieval points, seems far and away the more crucial aspect.

Having relegated cataloging fullness to second place, however, does not mean it is acceptable to ignore persistent problems in access to serials. Serials cataloging usually contains little information, because catalogers omit elements that change over time and leave blank spaces for final issue numbers, etc. I never knew a patron who wanted a whole serial run, but library catalogers are interested solely in whole runs. To be cataloged as a serial is to eliminate most of the elements used to identify, locate, and select materials for use, such as authors' and editors' names, article titles, the representation of contents through indexing and classification, and, even, a full description of the physical material itself.[8] The Library of Congress, which sets the standard for quality cataloging practice, uses the simplest and least informative bibliographic model, the *Anglo-American Cataloguing Code's* level 1, for describing serials. Details given in the catalog record relate solely to the title's first issue or, when that is not available, the earliest issue in the library's possession. Consider how helpful that kind of catalog record is today for a scientific journal that began publishing in the 19th century, or for an e-journal that publishes daily or weekly.

Standard practices dictate that elements expected to change from issue to issue of serials are eliminated from the catalog records prepared by libraries. Instead, commercial organizations are entrusted to provide access to the contents. (I call this doing the cataloging, but others disagree.) Patrons get a pointer from the library catalog indicating the library owns a title, but no more. They must go to a non-library-produced index to find a desired work (an article, column, editorial, chapter, or review) and note its location in detail (volume, issue, pages); compare that against the library's holdings list to see if the desired part is, indeed, in the library's collections; and, if it is, go to the shelf hoping to find the material. These hopes are occasionally dashed, but most of the time patrons do succeed. The electronic universe has similarities–the desired item could be outside the library's contract or limited to selected subscribers.

Fortunately, this scenario is changing, thanks to the capabilities of library computers. Holdings records are often attached to bibliographic records, enabling the catalog to show if a desired part of a serial is available. But it still seems too difficult for libraries to do more than minimal descriptions or to apply subject indexing to serial parts smaller than the entire publication–all issues and all text, past, present, and future. Following the model of the monographic book, which mandates summarizing the entire item as the chosen unit for subject indexing with a handful of descriptors, serials have fared poorly in standard cataloging operations. Instead of providing intellectual access, library catalogs provide inventory control, something librarians would never tolerate as sufficient for the monographic books they buy.

WHAT ELSE IS MISSING?

The principal problem I see with the way librarians approach cataloging is that we still start with the material and take from that material what we think is needed by patrons. Common sense dictates that we need to gather bibliographic information for identification purposes and that it should be gathered from the materials being cataloged, and I would never try to suggest we stop doing it. But we know this process does not completely fulfill our obligation to make materials available to patrons. We should progress to the point where we start with patrons and ask how to make what they need accessible from the material. To do this means beginning with studies that reveal how patrons search, the psychological effects of different access routes and delivery systems, and how various metadata systems are interpreted by patrons at different levels of expertise. Then, taking what can be learned from such studies, we can reinterpret cataloging objectives in patron-centered terms that might produce different results from those of our traditional cataloging systems. As an ivory-tower inhabitant, I will make some wild predictions at this point: if we start from the user's perspective instead of from the material's perspective, we will have to revise our ideas about what should be cataloged and how the cataloging should be delivered, at the very least, and also how the data should be formulated and presented.

Standard cataloging practice refuses to delve beneath summary-level in providing access, although we know catalog records are used to select materials to answer a searcher's needs. Do patrons always seek a whole title, or, do they often seek only parts of it? I believe what we do in cataloging serials is similar to a realtor trying to sell a house without letting the buyer peek inside at the layout and the rooms. Who would commit $250,000 or more to buy a house based solely on its identification as a "modular Cape Cod on one-quarter of an acre of land, seven rooms, grey with forest green shutters and trim, at 822.33 Stratford-upon-Avon Road"? What if my requirements for a house include having a bedroom on the first floor or a full bath in the attic? The description I gave would not tell me if this house answered my needs. Catalog records have pretty much the same limited revelatory power compared to what patrons wish to know. (For that matter, bindings are rarely mentioned, which might be more valuable information for searchers seeking an item they know has an unusual binding than the number of pages or the presence of illustrations.)

In a traditional environment in which onsite searching of a limited nature was the rule, the selection function of the catalog could be satisfied with a few simple specifications and descriptors giving a brief outline of contents. Patrons could go to the shelves and see what was there or consult other reference sources to define the details. Patrons could take materials in hand, leaf through them, scan tables of contents or abstracts, and decide on the spot if they wanted them. Today, however, users are likely to be located far from library buildings. They must rely entirely on what catalog records say to decide whether to initiate a sometimes costly, sometimes complicated request to obtain an item. If the item turns out to be less relevant than expected, or less complete, less authoritative, or less accurate, can we truly say the material disappointed them? Or, should we own up to the true culprit, the catalog record, whose information lacked the detail needed to answer the searcher's simple question, "Is this what I want?"

Since the advent of computers, when it became clear that catalogers could work from terminals located anywhere in their libraries, not solely in a cataloging room, I wondered why this large, knowledgeable group of experts never moved out into the reference area, offering to interpret the catalog directly to searchers instead of allowing it to be filtered through others, or not filtered at all. Think of the game of "Telephone," in which the first person in a large group whispers a phrase into the ear of his or her neighbor, who whispers it to another, and on around a large group of people. When the last person shouts the phrase aloud, the reaction is, inevitably, a roar of laughter on hearing how the words have been revised and garbled during their passage among the participants. Similarly, while catalogers may believe they create clear, precise catalog records after they are seen and interpreted by others, they tend, just as inevitably, to be altered in the process. If I search for something in Library X's catalog via the Web, and cannot tell if it meets my needs, I might ask a reference librarian for help. If that librarian is not certain of the material's value to me, he or she might consult the holding library's reference librarian, who must interpret both my need and the relationship to my need of the material represented by the catalog record, which he or she did not create. I cannot interact with the creators of catalog records or make my decision with the fewest opportunities for garbling either my message or that of the catalog record. We seem to have lost our way in a maze of specialization to a point where the expertise needed to resolve searchers' problems is always beyond our reach.

Just as computers and automation have blurred the lines between the administrative distinctions of technical and public services, they blur the intellectual distinctions between cataloging and reference. It is more important than ever that both kinds of librarians be experts in bibliographic control and access, and that both kinds of librarians use their knowledge to serve the public. As a cataloging educator for twenty years with eighty to one hundred students a year, I see some preparing for jobs in reference who allow the details of standard cataloging practice to slip quietly into oblivion once they have passed my course. As educators, we do a poor job of impressing on them the importance of interpreting the catalog, or how difficult and intellectually demanding it is. Yet, we give them their degrees and send them out into the world to practice, where they can substitute conjecture for rock-solid knowledge when it comes to the catalog. But I digress.

The advent of one-stop shopping in full-text databases, connecting a patron searching for bibliographic elements directly with documents, demands we stop looking at resources as fodder for bibliographic databases and start looking at them as a set of holistic choices that patrons select. Cataloging is no longer separate from the material it describes. It is part of the material now and must advertise its contents to the greatest extent possible, because librarians are no longer an integral part–albeit a behind-the-scenes-part–of the retrieval process.

LOOKING FOR INSPIRATION

Libraries occupy a position in the world of knowledge that does not differ a great deal, metaphorically speaking, from the position of department stores and other retail shops in the world of consumer goods. Librarians buy the intellectual and artistic products of many publishers and producers, and offer them to members of the public who come looking for these goods. Like retailers, librarians buy materials for different audiences and for different purposes. Yet, library transactions, like those of retail stores, are to individuals one-at-a-time, and carry no guarantees they will continue to come back. We might think of big city central libraries and large university research libraries as the Macy's of the intellectual world; small-town libraries and college libraries are the general stores; some academic and numerous special libraries are the boutiques, purveying smaller numbers of high quality specialty items rather than general merchandise at mid-level quality and mid-level prices.

Just as there were few alternatives years ago to department stores, general stores, and boutiques if one wanted to buy consumer goods, there were few alternatives to library collections and services for readers who did not care to or could not afford to buy the intellectual goods. In those days, store owners believed they only had to open their doors and the public would come to buy. Librarians also believed they only had to open their doors and offer their collections in order to please the public, and, I fear, catalogers believed they only had to please other librarians. Times, however, have changed. Now, there are many convenient alternatives both to department stores and libraries. Librarians in all specialties have a new imperative to please readers and persuade them to continue coming back to their libraries. I suggest we might look to successful retailers for new ideas about how to do it, especially to those aspects of merchandising they use to sell goods to retail customers and turn them into repeat customers.

Think about what happened over the last half-century to downtown flagship department stores when shoppers began moving to the suburbs. How did they change to survive? Many didn't, of course, but those that did often decentralized–moved to the suburbs and became mall anchors–or switched to direct sales through catalogs, or combined their buying power by amalgamating. Some became mass marketers–national chains such as WalMart, Borders, Starbucks–or mass distributors, like Land's End and L. L. Bean. They employed a variety of strategies to identify, reach, and expand their markets. Among other things, they spent a great deal of time and money researching and developing their markets, hiring professionals who conducted mass surveys and focus interviews, ran tests and experiments, and analyzed demographic patterns. They learned who their potential markets were, profiled their tastes, and tailored their offerings to match. Some stores succeeded by filling particular niches, each developing a unique image and a sense of "message." They advertised, using all kinds of advertising systems, old and new, to communicate–newspapers, magazines, broadcast radio, network television, cable systems, satellite systems, and the Internet. They promoted "lost leaders"–goods sold well below market value that would attract buyers to the store–and recouped their losses by arranging their wares on the selling floor in ways that made customers pass as many tempting counters as possible before reaching their destinations. Salespeople cooperated by encouraging potential buyers to "step up" and buy more costly, higher quality items, and were rewarded with larger commissions when they succeeded.

Three new strategies were added to this already imposing list: (1) competitive intelligence–the in-depth research of whole industries and concomitant positioning of a retailer within its cohort of competitors; (2) customzation–offering services such as monogramming or mix-and-match options (the way one might buy a new car); and (3) bundling–selling a product with numerous related items added in to the total package. Consumers are wooed and won with convenience, advertising, service, price, and plenty of market research, and competition is fiercer than ever.

The ranks of e-commerce enterprises, such as Amazon.com, offer deeper insights into new ways to merchandise consumer goods. There is no simple transaction at Amazon. A potential buyer is flooded with prompts to buy, tempted by special offers, urged by the positive comments of other buyers, and hustled through a forest of excellent auxiliary services to a plethora of commodities, available at the click of one's mouse. Every time I visit Amazon, I have to be careful where I point my mouse, alert that some stray move might pop something into my marketbasket and onto my credit card before I realize what I've done. Yet I go back time after time, because Amazon rarely disappoints me, and often what I want is only a survey of the marketplace of books or videos on a subject, not a specific purchase. Amazon never tells me to go away until I am ready to buy, or stigmatizes me as a "window shopper." Every time I log on, Amazon is as happy as ever to welcome me, eagerly offering new bargains, specials, and bonuses for my patronage.

MARKETING A LIBRARY'S INTELLECTUAL GOODS

The catalog is one of the two principal links between a library and its readers, the other being its public service librarians. The catalog has a much greater capacity than librarians working within a library building of reaching both onsite and offsite readers, and it frequently is the gateway to outside resources acquired on behalf of the readers. I believe it is impossible to overestimate the significance and value of the catalog for today's readers, whether they are cardholders in our libraries or not; whether the libraries are part of academic, community, or corporate organizations; and whether the materials involved are accessed online or through methods designed to transport non-electronic materials.

Furthermore, I believe the current environment–Web-based resources, including increasing numbers of e-journals, forming an overabundant supply of raw material, diverse kinds of patrons with ever-more-diverse information needs, frequent blurring of disciplinary boundaries, and search practicalities that lack either the time or the logistics for continuing to employ traditional access methods effectively–dictates a fundamental shift in our thinking about serials cataloging. We must ask how to make the catalog provide more useful information about the things searchers seek–which will rarely be an entire e-serial–and give a lot more personal service via librarian interfaces with patrons at the point of their search–not through some standard but limited precoordinated set of options that patrons have to learn by participating in years of bibliographic instruction sessions.

Some observers see this as a gender-related issue. An article appearing some months ago in *The New York Times* special section on e-commerce stated, "Women are looking for different information and in different ways from the traditional male audience, forcing Web site designers to rethink their products . . . Hifi.com has introduced Herhifi.com, which sells the same stereos and televisions as the original Web site but in a different way. Links to a plain-spoken expert are displayed prominently. And, instead of listing products in traditional categories like home theater or video, with emphasis on the gadget, Herhifi.com emphasizes context, selling products by room, like kitchen and home office. Sites that cater to women generally have more prominent search tools, links to chat rooms and forums or other places where the users can ask questions–features that female Web users in surveys say more sites should adopt. 'Designers should consider moving from a broadcasting model of communication to an interactive and dynamic palette where users are collaborators . . .'"[9]

I never thought of library catalogs as having a "broadcasting model of communication," but it explains what is wrong with traditional cataloging in a Web-based world. In my opinion, accommodations to "female" search psychology on the part of several e-firms suggest ways to improve serials cataloging operations and enable the catalog to do a better job of rewarding patron search efforts. We can provide more prominent search tools, multiple approaches to the representations of both descriptive and subject content (such as Herhifi.com's listings by function as well as by location), and, most of all, we can supply a link to a plain spoken expert to whom baffled searchers can turn for advice. Every time someone initiates a catalog search session for the first time, they should be prompted to consult with a plain spoken expert–namely, a librarian–just as one is prompted to buy the latest offering to an Internet Service Provider's subscribers during the first login of the day. One can always say "no." The librarian-advisor–whether he or she spends most of a workday in the library at a public desk answering questions, or selecting, acquiring, and organizing new materials at a backroom workstation–should stand ready to suggest effective search strategies and help when expected responses fail.

These suggestions go beyond mere bibliographic data to bibliographic services. Once, the primary bibliographic service rendered by any library to its patrons was preparation of the catalog; but today, we need to think more broadly. I believe we must change our ideas about what constitutes a valid bibliographic unit. We need to stop cataloging complete entities and start focusing on what patrons seek. Nor is this the first time we have faced the issue. Microform sets posed a similar problem for catalogers, because one physical carrier contained numerous works. Traditional bibliographic units encompassing whole sets simply did not furnish an appropriate level of access to what was in the set. New levels of analysis had to be considered and compromises reached. Perhaps, for Web-based resources, we should go deeper still, turning catalog records into brief back-of-the-book indexes, parsing and representing the ideas–not the sites–on the Web.

To sum up, we can attempt to translate what has succeeded in the world of commerce into equivalent terms appropriate to cataloging and classification. We, the creators of the catalog, can try to reach out to patrons and serve them better, making it worth their while to continue consulting us and using our libraries. We can and should employ graphic interfaces, especially to identify visual materials; illustrate the resources we offer; provide floor plans and maps in addition to call numbers; give teasers, free samples, bonuses and credits to patrons; reward frequent users; and go to deeper bibliographic levels to describe and evaluate resources. We can piggyback marketing messages onto retrieval sets and offer hot buttons for circulation, acquisition, interlibrary loan, and related research services. In effect, the catalog can offer a whole range of library services to searchers, not solely indicate the presence or absence of a particular item in a library's collections.

CONCLUSION

Catalog records, particularly for electronic serials, are no longer one of many fully-mediated steps in a patron's search process, but the one and only opportunity to point patrons in the right direction to satisfy their information needs. To do this, we have to strike new balances between uniformity and flexibility. While uniformity fosters wide interchangeability–something we have prized highly, and rightfully so–it strictly limits individuality–something the current environment demands. Where should a new equilibrium be set? What can help us to decide?

First, we need to determine how predictable and stable client needs are. The fewer variations we must support–such as external campuses and distance learning students; patrons of peer libraries, consortia, regional cooperatives, and others; and totally unaffiliated patrons from here and abroad–the more stable and predictable are the sum of patron needs, and the more we should lean toward maintaining uniform standards. The more diverse our patron populations and the more we wish to customize our services to them, the more productive flexibility becomes.

Second, we need to know how fluid the institutional environment is. Those who can support flexibility should do so, positioning themselves better for the future. Those who cannot do so yet should work toward such capabilities, because the future is very likely to require greater flexibility.

Third, what strengths and weaknesses do current operations exhibit? Knowing them and reviewing them with regard to the advantages and disadvantages of uniformity versus flexibility, we can design systems that foster appropriate change.

What seems clear is that we need to expand bibliographic offerings to an increasingly diverse client base and do more work for patron-searchers than ever before. Metadata–which is evolving into a broad, collaborative effort involving many segments of society, many countries and languages, and varied methods of accessing desired information–offers new options. Perhaps, metadata can take us beyond the catalog as a collection of surrogates to the catalog as a true guide to knowledge.

What is happening to librarians is not unique. It is happening outside of libraries to every other organization involved with human beings and the Internet. We can learn from what we see happening around us. At the very least, we can:

- engage patrons as individuals
- serve them with our professional knowledge

- use technology to expand bibliographic data and service options
- seek to achieve broader and deeper levels of control in order to accommodate a growing diversity of informational materials, information needs, and information seekers.

Resting on our traditional laurels will earn us a slippery slide into obsolescence. Taking hold of our traditional tools and reshaping them to address new questions might help to assure our continued relevance and develop a following of satisfied clients who return to their libraries' catalogs again and again.

AUTHOR NOTE

Dr. Sheila S. Intner is a Professor in the Graduate School of Library & Information Science at Simmons College and Director of GSLIS at Mount Holyoke College, its master's degree program in western Massachusetts. Dr. Intner teaches and conducts research in the area of cataloging and collection development; and she also teaches professional writing, bibliographic instruction, basic materials repair, and intellectual freedom. Winner of the 1989 OnLine Audiovisual Catalogers Award, the 1992 Brubaker Award, and the 1997 Margaret Mann Award for outstanding contributions to cataloging and classification, she has published 16 books, including *Standard Cataloging for School and Public Libraries*, now in its third edition, as well as numerous articles and chapters in books. She also edits the monographic series *Frontiers of Access to Library Materials* for ALA Editions and writes the bimonthly "Dollars and Sense" column for *Technicalities*. Among her service activities, Dr. Intner has been elected Chair of OnLine Audiovisual Catalogers, Chair of the Cataloging & Classification Section of the Resources & Technical Services Division of the American Library Association, President of the Association for Library Collections & Technical Services, and an American Library Association Councilor. She spent a year in Israel as a Senior Fulbright Professor to Israel.

REFERENCES

1. Sheila S. Intner and Jean Weihs, *Standard Cataloging for School and Public Libraries*, 3rd ed. (Englewood, CO: Libraries Unlimited, 2001).

2. For reasons why I believe this to be true, see my chapter in Bella Hass Weinberg's *Cataloging Heresy*, "Rejecting Standard Cataloging Copy: Implications for the Education of Catalogers" (Learned Information, 1992, pp. 119-130).

3. Six academic library directors interviewed recently estimated the proportion of their collections in electronic resources was between 15% and 30%. They forecast a slow but steady increase to between 30% to 40% in the next several years. The full report of the study is found in Sheila S. Intner, "Impact of the Internet on Collection Development: Where Are We Now? Where Are We Headed? An Informal Study," *Library Collections, Acquisitions, & Technical Services* 25 (2001): pp. 307-322.

4. *Cataloging Heresy*, p. 119.

5. Charles A. Cutter, *Rules for a Dictionary Catalog*, 4th ed. (Washington, DC: Government Printing Office, 1904), p. 12.

6. S. R. Ranganathan, *The Five Laws of Librarianship* (Bombay: Asia Publishing House, 1963).

7. Marshall McLuhan, *Understanding Media, the Extensions of Man* (New York: McGraw-Hill, 1964), p. vii, 7-21.

8. I have written about this issue at some length. See Sheila S. Intner, *Interfaces: Relationships Between Library Technical and Reference Services* (Englewood, CO: Libraries Unlimited, 1993), pp. 77-92.

9. Steven E. Brier, "Since Women Ask for Directions, the Web Is Being Remapped," *The New York Times*, Special Section on "E-commerce" (Wed., Mar. 29, 2000).

AACR2 and Other Metadata Standards:
The Way Forward

Ann Huthwaite

SUMMARY. Changes in the environment in which the *Anglo-American Cataloguing Rules*, second edition (AACR2), currently operates are examined, including the growth in electronic publishing and use of the Internet, and the development and increasing use of a range of other metadata standards, such as the Dublin Core.

AACR2 and other metadata standards, particularly the Dublin Core, are compared. It is argued that AACR2 should continue to be used for describing selected Web-based resources. Criteria for deciding whether to use AACR2 or another metadata standard are defined, drawing on the experiences of two Brisbane universities in developing mechanisms for provid-

Ann Huthwaite is Library Resource Services Manager, Queensland University of Technology, Level 6, R Block, Kelvin Grove Campus, Brisbane, State of Queensland, Australia (E-mail: a.huthwaite@qut.edu.au).

The article was transcibed by Steven Jack Miller, Head, Monographs Department, University of Wisconsin-Milwaukee Libraries.

[Haworth co-indexing entry note]: "AACR2 and Other Metadata Standards: The Way Forward." Huthwaite, Ann. Co-published simultaneously in *Cataloging & Classification Quarterly* (The Haworth Information Press, an imprint of The Haworth Press, Inc.) Vol. 36, No. 3/4, 2003, pp. 87-100; and: *Electronic Cataloging: AACR2 and Metadata for Serials and Monographs* (ed: Sheila S. Intner, Sally C. Tseng, and Mary Lynette Larsgaard) The Haworth Information Press, an imprint of The Haworth Press, Inc., 2003, pp. 87-100. Single or multiple copies of this article are available for a fee from The Haworth Document Delivery Service [1-800-HAWORTH, 9:00 a.m. - 5:00 p.m. (EST). E-mail address: docdelivery@haworthpress.com].

10.1300/J104v36n03_08

ing access to electronic resources. Five options are evaluated: catalog only (direct entry); catalog only (indirect entry); subject gateway only; catalog and subject gateway combined; and shared databases, such as CORC. The option chosen by the two universities is identified and explained.

Revisions to the rules in AACR2 for cataloging electronic resources resulting from decisions made through 2000 are described. Possible future revisions are also explored. *[Article copies available for a fee from The Haworth Document Delivery Service: 1-800-HAWORTH. E-mail address: <docdelivery@haworth press.com> Website: <http://www.HaworthPress.com> © 2003 by The Haworth Press, Inc. All rights reserved.]*

KEYWORDS. AACR2, Dublin Core, cataloging, subject gateways, CORC, Websites

The *Anglo-American Cataloguing Rules*, second edition (AACR2), are a metadata standard that remains as viable today as any of the other metadata standards being used to organize electronic information. This is especially true as its rules are being revised to accommodate changes in the current information environment. To provide a background for looking more closely at AACR2 as a viable metadata standard, it is useful to start by considering the important environmental changes and the impact they are having on libraries and information organizations.

ENVIRONMENTAL CHANGES

First, we have witnessed tremendous growth in the Internet. The rise of the Internet has redefined what we mean by "information." Information has become ubiquitous, seeping into our homes and our lives–we are awash with it. Users grapple with an information explosion and unmanageable quantities of useless information. They increasingly need filters to help them cope. We see a growing recognition that information on the Internet must be organized in order to be useful. This environment presents enormous opportunities for information specialists, including catalogers, if we can grasp these opportunities in time.

In addition to the growth of the Internet, we are experiencing a proliferation of the variety of information media. In the past, information formats were clearly defined and recognizable, but now the boundaries between them are much more fluid. For example, in the past a "computer file" was always a physical object; now an "electronic resource" can exist in either tangible/direct-access form or intangible/remote-access form, without any physical item-in-hand available to the cataloger. Remote-access electronic resources are unstable, moving across boundaries. They can be elusive creatures that seem to defy description.

We are also experiencing changes in the expectations of information users. Increasingly, they expect immediate access to information. This has become an era of instant gratification. People want to gain maximum effect with minimum input. Information gathering is no longer an arcane exercise occurring within library walls; it occurs every day within people's homes and offices.

In response to the recognition that electronic resources must be organized in order to be retrievable, rapid growth has taken place in the number of different metadata standards being used for such organization. AACR2 has never had a monopoly on resource description. Other metadata standards have always been available for information users, such as those employed by abstracting and indexing services, operating in a part of the information universe beyond the library catalog. New metadata standards, such as the Dublin Core, have now been spawned in different domains.

A final environmental factor to take into account is globalization. Advances in communication and transportation mean that national barriers are being bypassed as we move into a world in which successful economies depend on international trade and resource sharing. Library cataloging has long been a global activity, which has led to its success. It has now become an imperative for cataloging to internationalize its activities.

AACR2 AND DUBLIN CORE

The changes in the current information environment described above have led to new situations for cataloging and resource description. The Dublin Core Metadata Initiative has emerged as one of the more significant alternative metadata standards for libraries. In recent years, many libraries have adopted Dublin Core metadata for use on a relatively wide scale. Australia and Scandinavia are two areas of particularly intense activity for Dublin Core. In Australia, variations of Dublin Core are being used for government material (e.g., the Australian Government Locator Service), educational information (e.g., Education Network Australia), subject gateways (e.g., the Australasian Virtual Engineering Library gateway to engineering information), and instructional material at universities. Growth in the number and variety of Internet resources has made it increasingly impractical for libraries to use AACR2 to describe all of them. "Cataloging the Internet," in the sense of creating traditional cataloging data for all resources on the World Wide Web, is an impossible task. But even when considering resource description solely for selected electronic resources, we should think in terms of using AACR2 for only some of them. In general, AACR2 should be used for "resources of continuing importance." Dublin Core offers a good choice for electronic resources that have been selected as useful, but are ephemeral or have a less essential level of importance as judged by resource selectors. Such a practice is supported in arguments presented by Michael Gorman,[1] who proposes four levels of bibliographic control for selected resources: (1) full cataloging using AACR2 and MARC; (2) enriched Dublin Core; (3) minimal Dublin Core; and, (4) leaving any remaining untreated materials to the search engines. Libraries and information centers need to be able to identify resources of continuing importance to be given full cataloging.

What advantages are there to using AACR2 as the metadata standard for describing resources of continuing importance? First, it is an international standard that continues to grow in use throughout the world. It is used in most English-speaking countries and has been translated into a number of other languages. Every year, the list grows longer. As a standard held in common by so many libraries worldwide, AACR2 has made widespread sharing of catalog records possible. Sharing catalog records and purchasing them from bibliographic networks such as OCLC (Online Computer Library Center) have made the use of AACR2, coded in MARC format, an economic imperative for many libraries.

Another advantage of AACR2 is that it is intended for all formats. AACR2 has been designed for description of all types of information resources, not just Internet resources, and can be used in a hybrid environment in which databases of records describe a broad range of resource types, including print, electronic, and other types of media. There is little evidence to indicate that print materials will disappear. On the contrary, every indication is that the hybrid multimedia environment will continue for the foreseeable future. AACR2 provides for integration of electronic resources into this hybrid environment. Today's information users want, even require, "one stop shopping." They do not want to have to consult a variety of catalogs and lists to locate resources. The AACR2-based catalog can provide it. Often users do not know at the outset what type of resource they want. They seek information, not a particular format.

AACR2 is a more precise standard than Dublin Core and many other metadata standards. Keyword searching works well some of the time, but if precision is important, only AACR2 can help guarantee that a searcher will be able to identify the desired resource precisely. Other metadata developers are discovering the value of this kind of precision and they are being drawn to more detailed methods of resource description.

AACR2 is also a more controlled metadata standard. AACR2's rules are tightly controlled by a single committee, namely, the Joint Steering Committee for Revision of AACR (JSC). The JSC considers proposed changes very carefully–perhaps too carefully for some–before acting on them. When changes are made, libraries using the rules endeavor to comply with them, particularly the national libraries.

Another important factor is that AACR2 provides for authority control. The benefits of applying authority control to names and places can be critical in determining the relevance of retrieved items. AACR2 provides a workable system for controlled forms of names and places. There is no point in inventing a new system for authority control when this one functions so well.

Finally, AACR2 provides a principled approach for resource discovery. An information user searching a catalog assumes a set of operating principles that guide his or her search and that provide guarantees about the search results. For example, based on AACR2's principle of authorship, a user can be confident that the "author" of a work has a particular type of relationship with the work.

WHEN TO USE AACR2

Because there are so many electronic resources, it is not practical to use AACR2 for all of them. Criteria are needed to determine when to use AACR2 and when to use other standards, such as the Dublin Core. An example of guidelines for making this choice are those recently developed by a working group composed of members from two Brisbane university libraries, the Queensland University of Technology Library and Griffith University Library. The working group was formed to develop a collaborative mechanism for the creation of catalog records for Internet resources to be integrated into the catalogs of both libraries. The scope of the project includes free Internet resources and excludes electronic journals and other purchased electronic resources.

The collaborative mechanism is intended to replace a subject-based gateway, which, for a number of reasons, was perceived as not working effectively. After discussion by stakeholders in both university libraries, the decision was made to store records in the catalogs instead of the external gateway. Reference librarians will create the records, completing Web forms for brief records based on the Dublin Core. The results of the form will be converted into MARC format for loading into the two catalogs using the standard crosswalk from Dublin Core to MARC. Personal and corporate authors from these items will not be part of the name indexes. They will only be searchable as keywords. Reference librarians will also be able to flag selected records for upgrading to full cataloging by the libraries' catalogers.

The working group developed a set of guidelines to assist the reference librarians in making decisions about which records should be upgraded to full-level cataloging. The process of developing the guidelines itself became an interesting exercise, because it required members of the group responsible for cataloging standards to think deeply about what value full cataloging can add. The guidelines have two general principles for the reference librarians to bear in mind when making their decision:

- Is there a need for a more precise description to enable greater precision in searching?
- Is there need for a more comprehensive description to enable all the elements found in a fully cataloged record to be included?

The guidelines further specify three aspects that the reference librarians should consider when making their decisions:

1. *Access points*: Selectors should consider cases in which standardized access points may be important. This could apply to resources in which the issuing corporate body is of paramount importance. Possible examples are the official reports of committees and commissions, conference proceedings, and primary legal materials. It might also include resources for which the use of *Library of Congress Subject Headings* is required to provide standardized access.

2. *Integration with the rest of the collection*: Selectors should keep in mind cases in which integration with other resources is an important factor. For example, do similar resources exist in print form and are they already represented in the catalog with full cataloging? Does the resource supplement, or is it otherwise related to, an existing print resource, making consistency in description important? Does the resource belong to an important series when other titles in the series have been given full cataloging?

3. *Content of the resource*: The reference librarians are asked to consider whether the content of the resource justifies full cataloging. For example, does the resource have lasting significance, such as an important government publication? Is the coverage unique? Does it have local significance, and/or relevance to the needs of clients? Is the resource in a particular format, such as a map or music, that could benefit from specialized treatment? Is the resource an important reference tool? Each of these factors might influence the decision about using AACR2 for full cataloging.

COMPARING OPTIONS FOR ACCESS

The working group at the Brisbane libraries looked at several models for providing access to free Internet resources before recommending the one they finally chose. The group recommended a two-level standard:

- Full cataloging using AACR2 and *Library of Congress Subject Headings* for resources of lasting value;
- A brief, Dublin Core type of record for the remainder. Following are the five options they considered and some of the advantages and disadvantages of each.

1. *Catalog only (direct entry)*: In this model, all electronic resources selected for description are cataloged fully. Subject specialists identify resources for description and advise cataloging staff of the URL (Uniform Resources Locator) by e-mail or a Web-based form. Catalogers then do all the resource description. The advantages of this option are that it provides integration with other resources and one-stop shopping for information users; it makes use of the existing library system, thereby avoiding development costs; and it provides for effective resource retrieval. The major disadvantage is that it entails serious workflow implications for cataloging staff, namely, that there are not enough catalogers to do this level of work for all the resources selected, and that it has the potential to create a growing backlog of uncataloged resources.

2. *Catalog only (indirect entry)*: This was the option actually chosen by the working group after considering all five. In this model, subject specialist staff create brief records in a Web-based form external to the catalog for inclusion in the catalog. Brief records for resources of lasting value are flagged for full cataloging. Catalogers then convert the completed forms to MARC format for loading into the catalog. The ad-

vantages of this option are that it provides integration with other resources and a one-stop shopping portal to the Web; it is more practical than option 1, since some resources are not given full cataloging; subject specialist staff acquire a greater understanding of resource description; and it presents opportunities for collaboration between technical services and reference staff. The working group does not necessarily consider this to be the final option; they can still choose other options if the environment changes.

3. *Subject gateway only*: This was the model the libraries had used previously on a trial basis, but which had proved unsuccessful for a number of reasons. The subject gateway was not being used a great deal by students and staff, and reference librarians were concerned that the resources were not available in the catalog. In addition, reference librarians were not giving sufficient time to resource description because they were uncertain about the value of the project. Now there is general agreement that the public catalog should be the focus for access to all information resources.

4. *Catalog and subject gateway*: This model is, perhaps, the ideal situation. The chief advantage is that users can find Internet resources in two ways–either through the catalog or via subject gateways. The working group considers this option a possible future direction for the project. The selected resources are assigned broad subject headings that can act as a gathering device for that purpose if needed. In this model, reference librarians can also choose to use the catalog to select resources for their own subject gateways.

5. *Use of shared databases, such as OCLC's Cooperative Online Resource Catalog (CORC)*: The working group investigated CORC as an option and chose to reject it at this time, but they will continue to monitor it. They believe it may become the future direction of the project. The perceived advantages of this model are that it employs an existing mechanism for record creation and contributes to a cooperative international initiative. The perceived disadvantages include varying quality of current records in the CORC database, the fact that the database does not contain records for Australian resources, and that CORC is expensive, made even more so because of a poor exchange rate.

AACR2: RECENT REVISIONS

AACR2 remains a viable metadata standard today and is being actively revised to accommodate the current information environment more effectively. Several recent revisions to AACR2 are relevant to electronic resources, in particular, the new Chapter 9. The lead in updating cataloging rules for electronic resources was taken by the International Federation of Library Associations and Institutions (IFLA) when it revised the *International Standard Bibliographic Description for Electronic Resources* (ISBD (ER)), first published in 1997.[2] The Committee on Cataloging: Description and Access of the Association for Library Collections & Technical Services[3] subsequently undertook to prepare rule revisions to align the rules in AACR2 with the new ISBD (ER). A task force assigned to do the job agreed that while harmonization (the Committee's term for "alignment") was a desirable end, complete alignment was not possible or appropriate in all cases. The following recommendations were subsequently approved by the Joint Steering Committee and incorporated into the 2001 rule revision package.

1. *Chapter 9 renamed*: The most obvious change to AACR2 was renaming Chapter 9 "Electronic Resources," replacing the former title "Computer Files."

2. *New general material designation for Chapter 9 materials–"electronic resource"*: Along with the change in terminology from computer files to electronic resources, the general material designation has likewise been changed from "computer file" to "electronic resource." This is symbolic of the larger change within AACR2 and reflects the shift from physical entities alone to both physical and virtual entities.

3. *Expansion of the scope of Chapter 9*: The scope of Chapter 9 has been broadened to include materials with characteristics in other classes of material. This illustrates a significant change in what was previously the basic principle of description embodied in rule 0.24, namely, that the physical format of the item being cataloged dictated the way it was to be cataloged. The new rule 0.24 now instructs the cataloger to bring out all aspects of the resource being described, including its content, carrier (that is, its particular physical format), type of publication, bibliographic relationships, and whether it is published or unpublished. Interactive multimedia materials are included within the scope of Chapter 9. The revised chapter makes clear the distinction between direct access and remote electronic resources: direct access means that a physical carrier can be described and must be inserted into an appropriate device attached to a computer; remote access means that no physical carrier is available and access can only be provided by the use of an input-output device.

4. *New definition of "chief source"*: The chief source of information for electronic resources is now the resource itself, instead of the title screen. This change has been made in recognition of the fact that elec-

tronic resources are so diverse it is extremely difficult to specify a consistent source. Within the resource itself, formally presented evidence is preferred, and a list of examples for formally presented evidence now includes encoded metadata such as Text Encoding Initiative headers and metadata tags.

5. *Inclusion of relevant examples*: More current examples for contemporary electronic resources have been added to the revised Chapter 9, especially for remote access, networked, and interactive multimedia resources.

6. *Updating of terms in the glossary*: Terms in the glossary have been added and amended as necessary to reflect the foregoing changes.

7. *Closer links with Chapter 12*: The revised Chapter 9 for electronic resources was released prior to the release of a new Chapter 12 for "continuing resources" (the term that replaces "serial publications"). The link between the two chapters has been emphasized, however, because many electronic resources are also continuing resources.

At this writing, the Joint Steering Committee was prepared to consider a number of related proposals, described in the next section.

FUTURE REVISIONS

Possible future revisions of AACR2 that have particular relevance to electronic resources include the following:

1. *Elimination of area 3 for Chapter 9*: The Library of Congress has proposed that area 3 for electronic resources, a required descriptive area formerly called "file characteristics" and now known as "type and extent of resource," be eliminated from Chapter 9 or at least made optional. The Library of Congress believes this information should be recorded in the note area of the bibliographic record instead. The Committee on Cataloging: Description and Access established a task force on specific characteristics of electronic resources to examine this proposal. The task force was charged with examining the rules not only for type and extent of resource (area 3), but also for physical description (area 5), and related notes (area 7). As a starting point, the task force surveyed the cataloging community on the topic. Based on this input and their deliberations, they concluded that area 3 is not useful, that this information should instead be recorded in area 7, and that area 5 should not be used for remote access electronic resources. Because some members of the cataloging community have had objections to these conclusions, the Joint Steering Committee decided to maintain area 3 until further discussion could take place.

2. *Reorganization of Part I of AACR2*: The Joint Steering Committee commissioned Tom Delsey of the National Library of Canada to conduct an analysis of AACR2 using modeling techniques. The result was his report on "The Logical Structure of the Anglo-American Cataloguing Rules, Parts I and II."[4] Regarding Part I, he recommended that an alternative way of organizing the rules be explored, suggesting that an arrangement by descriptive area might be useful. This rearrangement may be helpful and improve usability, but it does not eliminate the class of materials concept. Specific rules for different classes of material would still be listed under the general rule for each area. Various constituencies reviewed a prototype of reorganized Part I, developed by Bruce Johnson and Bob Ewald of the Library of Congress, which was to be discussed.

3. *Strategies for dealing with format variation (that is, "multiple versions")*: One of the most fundamental problems with the current AACR2 is its inability to deal efficiently with multiple versions of the same work. The approach of AACR2 is embodied in rule 0.24, which implies that a new catalog record should be created when the same work appears in different physical carriers. The latest revision of rule 0.24 emphasizes the importance of bringing out all aspects of a resource, including both content and carrier. Catalogers must still, however, choose a primary class of material for a resource when cataloging it. This is a real problem in the electronic environment. Faced with multiple records for the same work, libraries are resorting to nonstandard alternatives, such as attaching the holdings of the electronic version to the record for the print version, thus allowing one record to represent both versions. The Joint Steering Committee has formed an international task force on format variation, chaired by Jennifer Bowen, to explore solutions to the problem. The group has been encouraged to look for a practical solution, one that the library community can support. They are developing an experiment to test the feasibility of creating bibliographic records based on "expressions" and whether information users could understand such records. Another task force of the Committee on Cataloging: Description and Access is working on an appendix containing explicit guidance on when to create new catalog records. In most instances, the appendix will reflect existing practice, therefore the work of this group is aimed at improving usability and clarity, not making fundamental changes to the rules.

4. *Examination of the role of general material designations*: The task force formed to examine the content versus carrier issue noted that the general material designation presents one of the most intractable barriers in attempting to resolve the content/carrier problem. The group agreed that the list of general material designations is riddled with contradic-

tions. For example, is a digital map a cartographic resource or an electronic resource? Should a cataloger have to choose? Can it be both? One proposed solution is to permit multiple general material designations. The general material designation terms, themselves, are not consistent. Some, such as "music," represent types of expressions, while others, such as "microform," represent types of manifestations (terms in quotations are derived from "Report on Functional Requirements for Bibliographic Records"[5]). Some members of the cataloging community ask whether general material designations should be abandoned altogether. A recent survey by Jean Weihs[6] addresses some of these questions. Barbara Tillett[7] also has examined the role of the general material designations. She suggests an option be explored to identify the mode of expression for information users, while terms representing the physical format or form of the carrier could be moved elsewhere, where they conceptually belong.

THE WAY FORWARD

The pace of rule revision has been accelerating since the International Conference on the Principles and Future Direction of AACR was held in 1997.[8] Current members of the Joint Steering Committee are dedicated to expediting the rule revision process. The Joint Steering Committee has become much more proactive in soliciting proposals, and has the support of its sponsor, the Committee of Principals of AACR, in pursuing efforts to speed up the process. They are now committed to a process of regular and rapid rule revision. The Joint Steering Committee is proceeding on a number of fronts, including: short-term revision to keep the rules relevant (e.g., revising Chapters 3, 9, and 12); making the rules more user-friendly (e.g., appendix on major changes, an expanded introduction, possible reorganization of Part I); and, exploration of a number of more fundamental issues (e.g., the format variation question, the content versus carrier issue).

The Joint Steering Committee has begun a program of work, with deadlines, for ensuring that they keep on track, and they are now planning an annual cycle of revisions. AACR2's publishers have agreed to make it a loose-leaf publication. The 2002 publication incorporates revised Chapters 3 and 12 (a new Chapter 9 was issued with other revisions in a package in late 2001). Then, it will subsequently be updated annually with insert pages. The goal is to make AACR2 itself a fully operational integrating resource.

The Joint Steering Committee intends to take a more strategic approach to rule revision. They find it increasingly necessary to take a holistic view, to avoid in effect, missing the forest for the trees. They will decide what AACR2 should be like in five years' time and which strategies they should employ to get there. The Joint Steering Committee intends to encourage research into new developments, involving testing and review. They recognize that AACR2 is one metadata standard among many. Therefore, it is important to keep the channels of communication open with other metadata communities, including communities responsible for International Standard Bibliographic Descriptions. Finally, the Joint Steering Committee intends to promote and market AACR2, conveying the message that it still has relevance. The current situation is not one of AACR2 and metadata, but rather of metadata including AACR2. AACR2 is not a standard to be contrasted with other metadata standards, but is itself a rich and viable metadata standard among the many available today for resource description.

AUTHOR NOTE

Ann Huthwaite is currently the Library Resource Services Manager at the Queensland University of Technology Library, where she is responsible for the cataloguing and acquisitions functions. She has been the Australian representative on the Joint Steering Committee for Revision of AACR (JSC) since 1994, and was appointed Chair of the Committee in 1999.

Ms. Huthwaite has a long involvement with cataloguing in Australia. She has been a member of the Australian Committee on Cataloguing since 1992, and was that committee's representative on the ABN Standards Committee. She was a joint editor of *Cataloguing Australia* for several years, and convened the 13th National Cataloguing Conference in 1999. She has served on the executive board of the Queensland Group of the ALIA Cataloguers' Section since 1987, generally as President of the Group.

Prior to her appointment at the Queensland University of Technology as the Cataloguing Librarian in 1989, Ms. Huthwaite worked in various positions at the State Library of Queensland. She holds a Bachelor of Arts degree and graduate diplomas in education and librarianship. She also holds a Master in Applied Science (Information Studies) from Charles Sturt University. The focus of her research for this degree was user interaction with the catalogue.

REFERENCES

1. Michael Gorman, "Metadata or Cataloging? A False Choice," *The Journal of Internet Cataloging* v. 2, no. 1 (1999): 5-22.

2. *ISBD (ER) = International Standard Bibliographic Description (Electronic Resources)* (London: UBC Programme, 1997).

3. This committee is charged with responsibility for AACR2 for the American Library Association, of which the Association for Library Collections & Technical Services is a division.

4. The report is available online from the Joint Steering Committee Web site at http://www.nlc-bnc.ca/jsc/docs.html.

5. Available online at http://www.ifla.org/VII/s13/frbr/frbr.pdf.

6. Available online at http://ublib.buffalo.edu/libraries/units/cts/olac/capc/gmd.html.

7. Available at http://www.nlc-bnc.ca/jsc/gmd.pdf.

8. *Proceedings of the International Conference on the Principles and Future Direction of AACR,* Jean Weihs, editor (Toronto: Joint Steering Committee for the Revision of AACR, 2001).

AACR2 and Metadata:
Library Opportunities
in the Global Semantic Web

Barbara B. Tillett

SUMMARY. Explores the opportunities for libraries to contribute to the proposed global "Semantic Web." Library name and subject authority files, including work that IFLA has done related to a new view of "Universal Bibliographic Control" in the Internet environment and the work underway in the U.S. and Europe, are making a reality of the virtual international authority file on the Web. The bibliographic and authority records created according to AACR2 reflect standards for metadata that libraries have provided for years. New opportunities for using these records in the digital world are described (interoperability), including mapping with Dublin Core metadata. AACR2 recently updated Chapter 9 on Electronic Resources. That process and highlights of the changes are described, including Library of Congress' rule interpretations.

KEYWORDS. Integrated library systems, cataloging, Functional Requirements for Bibliographic Records (FRBR), cataloging standards, AACR2, Semantic Web, Library of Congress

Barbara B. Tillett is Chief, Cataloging Policy and Support Office, Library of Congress, 101 Independence Avenue, SE, Washington, DC 20540-4305 (E-mail: btil@loc.gov).

[Haworth co-indexing entry note]: "AACR2 and Metadata: Library Opportunities in the Global Semantic Web." Tillett, Barbara B. Co-published simultaneously in *Cataloging & Classification Quarterly* (The Haworth Information Press, an imprint of The Haworth Press, Inc.) Vol. 36, No. 3/4, 2003, pp. 101-119; and: *Electronic Cataloging: AACR2 and Metadata for Serials and Monographs* (ed: Sheila S. Intner, Sally C. Tseng, and Mary Lynette Larsgaard) The Haworth Information Press, an imprint of The Haworth Press, Inc., 2003, pp. 101-119.

http://www.haworthpress.com/store/product.asp?sku=J104
10.1300/J104v36n03_09

INTRODUCTION

Through the ages human beings have communicated and recorded their knowledge. As technology advanced they captured their ideas using new tools (see Figure 1). They used clay tablets, then later pen and ink on scrolls. The Chinese and the Europeans used printing tools, first wood blocks, then printing presses, and eventually presses with movable type. Typewriters then came along and individual authors could produce their own print-like documents. When photocopiers were invented, they could make lots of copies to distribute to many people. With personal computers and now the Internet, the creation and distribution of the works of an author can be accomplished more easily than ever.

Library catalogs have also evolved with changes in technology. Early librarians kept inventories of their collections on clay tablets or on scrolls. When the codex format was established, librarians embraced that technology to create book catalogs and finding aids. Card catalogs emerged around the turn of the 20th century, and the Library of Congress began distributing its printed cards starting in 1901. Other libraries were then able to re-use the cataloging work done centrally. With the introduction

FIGURE 1. Changing Technology

Changing Technology

● Tools
  » **Clay tablets**
  » **Pen and ink on scrolls**
  » **Printing press**
  » **Typewriters**
  » **Photocopying**
  » **Computers**
  » **PCs**
  » **Internet**

● Catalogs
  » **Collection inventories**
  » **Book catalogs and Finding aids**
  » **Card catalogs**
    – LC's printed card sets
  » **Online catalogs**
    – Bibliographic utilities for shared resources
  » **Integrated library systems**

of personal computers, librarians quickly embraced the new technology to offer their catalogs online. Bibliographic utilities developed to offer shared bibliographic and authority records. Catalogs have now become an essential component in integrated library systems and with today's global Internet technology, online catalogs are part of even larger systems that include portals and gateways to digital resources in combination with the traditional library resources (see Figure 2).

Computer-based library systems started really taking off in the 1970s, building on records encoded in the MARC format, which began to be created in the late 1960s. By the 1990s most vendors had systems that fully integrated all library functions, using the bibliographic and authority records as a core source of data that could be shared for acquisitions, serials check-in, binding, cataloging, inventory control, circulation, and in the online catalog for reference purposes.

By the year 2000, more integration of tools was occurring, with some vendors offering products that provided an umbrella to organize and make accessible both the traditional collections and digital collections a library wished to offer its users.

FIGURE 2. Integrated Library Systems

Integrated Library Systems

- 1970s - automating basic library functions around a MARC record
- 1990s - integration of library functions & some links to a&i : acquisitions, serials check-in, binding, original and copy cataloging, authority control, shelflisting/ classification, inventory control, circulation, online catalog for reference,
- 2000s - more integration of library tools: digital and all other resources, in the Library and remotely accessed

The materials librarians catalog also continue to evolve as new technologies are introduced. The formats and the packaging (or carriers) continue to proliferate, and some come and go, like filmstrips and punched cards (see Figure 3).

Libraries have always selected what they feel their users need or what their users tell them they want. Everything is rarely cataloged, not even everything in a library. We rely on other tools to provide bibliographic control over some types of materials, for example, maps in a series with their own index, or technical reports indexed by commercial services. Relying on others for some of the bibliographic control is not a new thing.

With the proliferation of journal articles, libraries and publishers tried to work together at the end of 1800s to provide catalog records for each article published. After a few months, it was abandoned as being unprofitable. That led H. W. Wilson to produce his periodical indexes and, since then, many other specialized abstracting and indexing services emerged to cover the periodical and report literature.

Libraries use abstracting and indexing services, bibliographies, directories, and many other tools in reference sources to help find information

FIGURE 3. What Are We Cataloging?

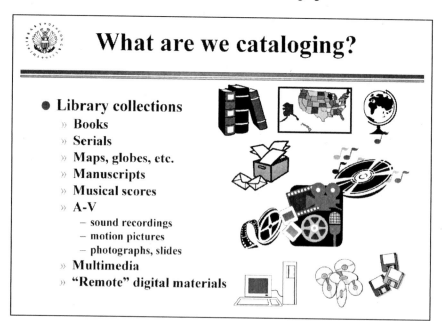

What are we cataloging?

● **Library collections**
  » **Books**
  » **Serials**
  » **Maps, globes, etc.**
  » **Manuscripts**
  » **Musical scores**
  » **A-V**
    – sound recordings
    – motion pictures
    – photographs, slides
  » **Multimedia**
  » **"Remote" digital materials**

that meets user needs. With the assistance of automation, we are integrating these tools with library catalogs to provide easier access for users.

EVOLUTION OF CATALOGING AND METADATA

The *Anglo-American Cataloguing Rules*, second edition, covers all types of materials, regardless of format or form. The basic rules are intended to apply to past, present, and future materials.

What is it that is actually being cataloged? A few years ago, a Study Group of the International Federation of Library Associations and Institutions (IFLA) issued a report that presented a conceptual model, called *Functional Requirements for Bibliographic Records* (FRBR) (see Figure 4).

In that conceptual model, the bibliographic universe was seen to consist of several related entities that could be described through data elements. The entities themselves were sorted into three groups as follows:

Group 1–Products of intellectual and artistic endeavor: work, expression, manifestation, and item

Group 2–Those responsible for the intellectual and artistic content: persons and corporate bodies

Group 3–The subjects of works: all of the above two groups as well as concepts, objects, events, and places.

The *Functional Requirements for Bibliographic Records* focused on Group 1, and a new IFLA working group titled Functional Requirements for Authority Numbers and Records continues developing this model, looking at Group 2.

Catalogers look at works that include other works (a recursive relationship) and at collections of items stored together when cataloging records or inventory control records are created, so they deal with "levels of granularity" and whole/part relationships.

The library world has a tradition of cataloging codes ("schemas" in current Web terminology). These national and international cataloging schemas build on cataloging principles and basic elements of description and access. They are based on internationally accepted standards, such as the Paris Principles and International Standard Bibliographic Descriptions. The standards are shared among libraries in many countries of the world today. Library cataloging schemas reflect a recognition of the importance of standards to facilitate sharing of bibliographic

FIGURE 4. Entities

Entities

● **FRBR entities**
  » **Group 1 entities (products of intellectual and artistic endeavor)**
   – Work
   – Expression
   – Manifestation
   – Item
  » **Group 2 (those responsible for the intellectual and artistic content)**
   – Person
   – Corporate Body
  » **Group 3 (subjects of works)**
   – All in Groups 1 and 2 plus:
   – Concept
   – Object
   – Event
   – Place

and authority records, the training of catalogers, and the achievement of consistency among many catalogers worldwide.

The standard elements and prescribed order of elements presented in our cataloging rules can be viewed as a metadata schema. AACR2 offers three levels of descriptions (rule 1.0D) plus another option for presenting data in a multilevel description (rule 13.6).

Other metadata schemas have developed such as the Committee on Scientific and Technical Information (COSATI) elements, Dublin Core (DC), the Encoded Archival Description (EAD), the Text Encoding Initiative (TEI), Online Information eXchange (ONIX–a schema being used by some publishers), and Visual Resources Association (VRA) for audiovisual materials. There are many more. IFLA has set up a Web page that identifies various metadata schemas. The IFLA Working Group on the Uses of Metadata Schemes is developing definitions and crosswalks (that is, matching tools) among the various schemas in an effort to recommend some basic elements that should always be provided in any metadata schema (see Figure 5).

FIGURE 5. Cataloging Schemas/Descriptive Metadata Schemas

Cataloging Schemas/ Descriptive Metadata Schemas

- National and international cataloging schemas *(years of shared resources)*
  - » AACR2 incorporating ISBD format
  - » RAK, RICA, AFNOR, RKP
- Schemas from other communities *(individual needs)*
  - » COSATI, Dublin Core, EAD, VRA, ONIX, TEI, etc.

Why do librarians feel the need to provide cataloging for materials that are proliferating on the Web? Some believe they do not need to be cataloged–it would be like planning to catalog all phone calls and mail. Cataloging activities focus on those materials librarians select for use by target audiences.

It is assumed that a library has a target group of users with particular needs, that materials are purchased that will fulfill those needs, and that the catalog of the library should enable the users to find the materials they need (see Figure 6). This finding objective is accomplished through standards for description and access in our rules. The catalog should also collocate the works of an author, which requires the use of controlled vocabularies and leads to greater precision of searching. A catalog may also collocate bibliographic records for entities on a particular topic.

In the *Functional Requirements for Bibliographic Records*, user tasks are also addressed–things a user wants to do relative to the bibliographic universe: find, identify, select, obtain, and relate the materials they find to others that may be in the collection.

If one looks at the Dublin Core as a prime example of a metadata schema and sees how it compares to the *Anglo-American Cataloguing*

FIGURE 6. Objectives of Catalogs

 Objectives of Catalogs

● Cutter's objectives for the catalog
  » Finding - *description and access standards*
  » Collocating - *controlled vocabularies for precision of searching*

● FRBR user tasks
  » Find
  » Identify
  » Select
  » Obtain
  » [Relate]

Rules, one sees that AACR2 is actually a deliberative rule process. Dublin Core is a metadata schema that has no rules of its own for syntax or semantics, but, instead, relies on the rules of other systems (see Figure 7). It can be very flexible for use with different authoritative systems. Specific application profiles are being developed to provide some guidance, such as the one for libraries, but Dublin Core itself is quite open.

AACR2 is an international standard and is based on other international standards, such as the International Standard Bibliographic Descriptions (ISBDs). Dublin Core is emerging as its own standard and as a National Information Standards Organization (NISO) standard for metadata.

AACR2 was created to deal with all types of materials in all formats. Dublin Core originally was focused on texts and specifically excluded things like maps and nonbook materials when it began. There are attempts now to expand it further.

AACR2 prescribes authority control and transcription of information from the item being cataloged. Dublin Core allows both controlled and uncontrolled data, but was originally thought to be a means for creators of digital objects to document some basic information that would be

FIGURE 7. AACR2 and Dublin Core

 # AACR2 and Dublin Core

- **AACR2**
  - » **Deliberative rule process**
  - » **International standard**
  - » **Intended for all materials**
  - » **Authority control**
  - » **Bibliographic description and access**

- **Dublin Core**
  - » **Rules inherited**
  - » **Own standard**
  - » **Texts**
  - » **Controlled and uncontrolled**
  - » **Basic info at point of creation (digital title page)**

needed for description and access of the objects. Ideally this descriptive and access data would be provided automatically when a digital object was created–the software would just provide it–like Microsoft Word automatically fills in a suggested name for a file and the date it was created. This information can be used later for retrieving that object.

Cataloging using AACR2 is done after a work and its manifestation have been created. In the Web environment an automatic tool is needed to create basic descriptive metadata at the point an object is created. Whether this is Dublin Core or some other standard yet to emerge, I believe future tools will provide for this, just as publishers now provide a title page on printed books.

The metadata that will be part of every future digital object can then be re-used in library catalogs and by search engines worldwide. The Library of Congress has already started doing this with the Electronic Cataloging-in-Publication (ECIP) program, in which information is captured from publishers electronically, and automatically inserted into a MARC 21 record for basic bibliographic description and access.

AACR2 AND WEB RESOURCES

Although AACR is an international standard for bibliographic description and access and it is designed to accommodate all forms of materials, it has been criticized for not handling "changes" quickly. This was most noticeable with the Internet at the end of the 1990s. Web pages were springing up and more information was being made available on the Web. The Internet was a place for authors and distributors to make information available very quickly.

However, the cataloging rules already provided an international standard for all forms of materials. It provided guidance for creating a comprehensive description with controlled access to all types of materials and in a way that enabled the re-use of bibliographic records among libraries. When cataloging for electronic resources is expected to provide comprehensive descriptions, have controlled access points, and be able to be integrated with other library resources, the use of AACR is justified.

When new forms of materials appear, updates and revisions are made to the rules through a very deliberative process. The rules are based on principles and are not intended to provide case law for every situation.

The Joint Steering Committee does not want to make sweeping changes to rules too quickly. Change is usually very expensive for libraries to implement. Nor is it useful to make a change only to change it back again in a very short time period. An intentional involvement of all constituents assures that rule changes are made thoughtfully and carefully, fully considering the impact and user needs that would be met by the change.

In 1997, an *International Standard Bibliographic Description for Electronic Resources* (ISBD (ER)) appeared. The *Anglo-American Cataloguing Rules* had already started the rule revision process (see Figure 8). Many of the current revisions stem from work of an American Library Association task force, known as the CC:DA ISBD (ER)–AACR Harmonization Task Force. The task force started its work recognizing that complete harmonization with ISBD (ER) was neither possible nor appropriate. Their proposal included cases where ISBD (ER) text was incorporated verbatim, cases where it was substantially reworded, cases where a conscious decision was made not to bring forward ISBD (ER) issues, and in some cases, going beyond the provisions in ISBD(ER) altogether. The Joint Steering Committee has agreed to communicate with the ISBD Review Group in IFLA about changes to AACR, but an inevitable degree of "disharmony" is acceptable at any point in time, as AACR is constantly being updated, while the ISBDs follow a 5-year update cycle.

AACR has a revised Chapter 9 for electronic resources and adjustments were made throughout the rules. The new scope of the chapter reflects accommodation to the new types of materials, particularly Internet resources, also reflected in updated examples.

"Chief source" is now changed to be the entire item. The consequence of this change is that catalogers now must use judgment, and some catalogers don't handle that well, preferring instead to follow rules. In a shared environment for cataloging, having such freedom of cataloger's judgment leads to duplicate records, so it remains to be seen if this change holds up a few years down the road.

Terms in the glossary have been updated, such as "container," "disk," "direct/remote access," and "electronic resource," but the use of those terms over time should be watched. Even the term "electronic resources" is artificial–when I go to meetings about digital libraries, "electronic" has the meaning of small appliances like hair dryers or microwave ovens. Perhaps the term will evolve to "digital objects" or something new in a few years time. The constant revision cycle of AACR allows the code to adopt new terminology when that is appropriate and useful.

What other changes are coming for the *Anglo-American Cataloguing Rules*? One suggestion is to eliminate Area 3 for electronic resources. This is the place where file characteristics are given, for example, "Computer data in 1 file." Maybe that is not needed and that information should be given in the physical description area or in a note.

FIGURE 8. AACR2 Recent Revisions

AACR2 Recent Revisions

- Alignment with ISBD(ER) - 1997
- Chapter 9 renamed "Electronic Resources"
- New GMD "Electronic resource"
- Expansion and clarification of scope of ch. 9
- New definition of "chief source"
- Inclusion of relevant examples
- Updated terms in Glossary
- Ch. 12 updates to "Continuing Resources"

As part of the proactive stance of the current Joint Steering Committee, Tom Delsey was commissioned to make recommendations regarding the logical structure of the rules and how to improve upon that. The possible reorganization of Part 1 of the rules, covering description, is being explored to arrange it in the areas of ISBD description rather than separate rules for different types of materials. An initial prototype was created for comment, and it is clear from that prototype that such a reorganization will require a great deal of work, especially the editing and harmonizing of rules that now vary from chapter to chapter.

Another proactive initiative of the Joint Steering Committee involved establishing an international working group on format variation. They are testing the use of expression-based records to which are attached records for specific manifestations (in the terminology of the IFLA's *Functional Requirements for Bibliographic Records*). Their report is expected in 2003.

The Joint Steering Committee is also currently examining the general material designation (GMD) and exploring the use of a similar designator for the mode of expression (cartographic material, sound, video, still image, text, etc.) and moving the form of carrier to the specific material designation (SMD) where it belongs conceptually.

An appendix might be added to help codify the decision making process for when to make new bibliographic records. It would clarify what constitutes a major change requiring the creation of a new bibliographic record. This appendix is being drafted by another task force of the American Library Association's cataloging committee.

What about the future? AACR will continue to be updated (see Figure 9) through regular and deliberative rule revisions. Revised chapters for cartographic materials (Chapter 3) and for continuing resources will be issued. "Continuing resources" is the new title covering serials and integrating resources (Chapter 12).

A new "Introduction" to the rules is planned to give the objectives of catalogs today, the principles behind the cataloging rules, and general concepts that form the foundation for the rules. Relevant examples will continue to be added as new types of materials are created and terms in the Glossary will be updated.

At the October 2001 meeting of the Joint Steering Committee in Ottawa, a strategic planning exercise was conducted to give clear goals and steps to improve the rules for the future. Ideas continue to be studied, such as the use of an expression-based record, and the findings of such studies are tested and reviewed to improve the rules further.

FIGURE 9. AACR2–Future Revisions

AACR2 - Future Revisions?

- Elimination of Area 3 for chapter 9
- Reorganization of Part 1 (Delsey recommendation)
- Strategies for dealing with format variation
- Examination of role of GMDs
- Addition of Appendix on major changes

The Joint Steering Committee communicates with other metadata standard communities to build bridges. The chair of the Joint Steering Committee has launched a promotion and marketing campaign to get the word out that AACR is an international standard upon which millions of bibliographic and authority records have been created, and that it applies just as well to providing metadata for basic bibliographic control of digital materials and future objects that libraries and others wish to organize. AACR continues to be relevant to the user needs of today and tomorrow.

LIBRARY OF CONGRESS ACTIVITIES

The Library of Congress, as the national bibliographic agency for the United States, responds to changes in the rules by providing national decisions related to rule options, and in some cases, by providing further guidance on how to interpret the rules in our national context. These rule interpretations lead to greater consistency in applying the rules, which is important for a very large institution and for its partners who help create compatible bibliographic and authority records. These guidelines are not appropriate for a cataloging code, but are needed for training and daily guidance to catalogers seeking to provide bibliographic description and access in a consistent way.

The Library of Congress adopted the latest set of amendments, including the rules for electronic resources, on December 1, 2002. Print copies of the amendments and the full set of rules are available from the AACR publishers: American Library Association, Canadian Library Association, and (British) Library Association.[1]

Catalogers at the Library of Congress will find those updated tools in our *Cataloger's Desktop* product. A new documentation series is being developed for Library of Congress catalogers to incorporate the various series now proliferating in paper, e-mail, and Web locations. The new series will be accessible on the Cataloging Policy and Support Office (CPSO) Website and catalogers wishing a print copy of any guideline can print the page for themselves.

OTHER DIGITAL ACTIVITIES AT THE LIBRARY OF CONGRESS

At the Library of Congress, where we strive to provide consistency in our cataloging, we are still experimenting with alternatives and ways to provide bibliographic control and access for digital resources. During the 2000 Presidential campaign, the Library of Congress initiated a Web preservation project, later called MINERVA, that explored techniques for grabbing snapshots of Web sites, storing them for long-term preservation, and cataloging them and making them accessible online. The MINERVA project continues to be active, for example, preserving Web sites related to the September 11 terrorist attacks. The catalog records were created in OCLC's Cooperative Online Resource Catalog and are available in both Dublin Core and MARC 21 views. The Library has also had other digital projects such as the Bibliographic Enrichment Advisory Team (BEAT) for bibliographic control of digital objects in the areas of business and economics.

In 2000, the Library started a new service unit for strategic initiatives. This unit also is responsible for managing the $100 million that Congress allocated to distribute to non-government institutions and organizations to help further knowledge about preserving digital objects long-term. This is not money to digitize, as the American Memory project was, but a focus on things "born" digital or already in digital form that should be preserved for posterity. Part of the money was also for developing a national digital information infrastructure preservation program plan and one piece of that plan will be recommendations for metadata policy.

Many other digital initiatives are going on in the Library and in cooperation with other organizations, such as the Program for Cooperative Cataloging. The Library of Congress has representation on the group developing the Dublin Core and has recently taken on being the maintenance agency for the Metadata Encoding and Transmission Standard (METS), as is done for the MARC 21 format and, jointly with the Society of American Archivists, for Encoded Archival Description (EAD). We have close ties with IFLA and various European Commission EU projects, such as the Linking and Exploring Authority Files (LEAF) and INTERPARTY that are exploring models for authority control in today's Web environment.

INTERNATIONAL ACTIVITIES

The IFLA Section on Cataloguing has several active working groups dealing with bibliographic control for electronic resources. The Working Group on the Use of Metadata Schemes has posted a list of metadata schemas on IFLA's Web site, IFLANET. The ISBD Review Group continues to update the international standards for bibliographic description and work with the cataloging rule-making bodies to try to maintain harmonization among the rules and the ISBDs.

Within this past year both the IFLA working groups on Guidelines for Authority Records and References (GARR) and on the Form and Structure of Corporate Headings (FSCH) supported the development of a virtual international authority file. Several projects in Europe have offered prototypes of internationally shared authority information, such as the Project AUTHOR, the LEAF Project (focusing on the needs of archives), the <indecs> Project (focusing on the needs of rights management organizations), and INTERPARTY (a follow-on to <indecs> to include libraries, museums, and archives, with the publishers and rights management organizations).

The Library of Congress also is exploring several projects to test a virtual international authority file. One proposal is to link the personal name authority file of the Library of Congress and that of the Deutsche Bibliothek (DDB) in Germany. With the help of OCLC, the retrospective files will be merged and linked and a server created to harvest essential metadata and keep the links updated as new records are created and old ones maintained.

A VIRTUAL INTERNATIONAL AUTHORITY FILE

Many varying models could be imagined, but one of the most promising is the model we propose for the Library of Congress-Deutsche Bibliothek project. It uses the Open Archive Initiative protocols with a central server that harvests metadata from the national authority files.

This model may be the best approach in terms of record maintenance. The information in the server is refreshed whenever there are changes in the national files. This means the day-to-day record maintenance activities continue to be managed as they are now by the national bibliographic agency (or regional authority).

In one scenario we envision this shared international authority file being an integral part of a future "Semantic Web" [2] (see Figures 10 and 11). The idea is to make the Internet more intelligent for machine navigation rather than human navigation of the Web. It involves creating an infrastructure of linked resources and the use of controlled vocabularies, called "ontologies."

Here's where libraries have an opportunity to contribute to the infrastructure of the future Web–we already have controlled vocabularies in

FIGURE 10. Semantic Web-1

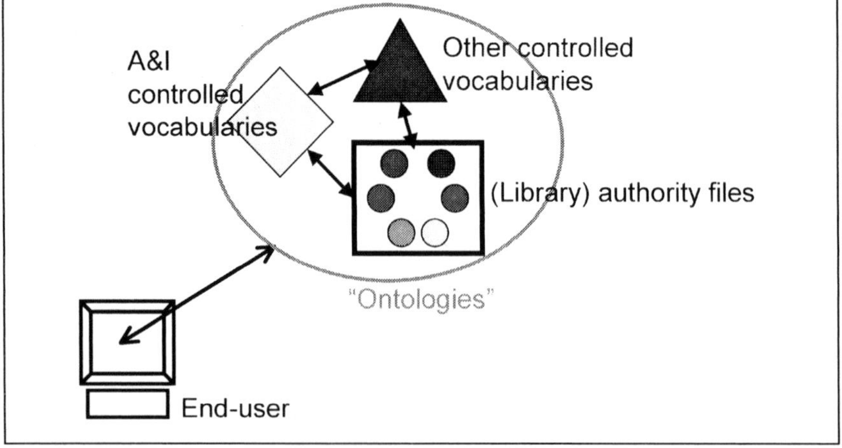

FIGURE 11. Semantic Web-2

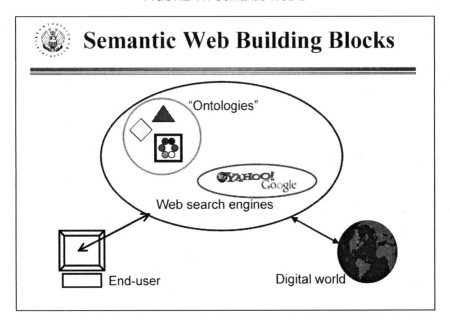

our various authority files. Those could be linked with other controlled vocabularies of abstracting and indexing services, of biographical dictionaries, of telephone directories, and many other reference tools and resources to help users navigate.

All of these tools would also link to their respective databases for bibliographic and other resources. For example, the Library of Congress authority files would link to the bibliographic and holdings databases of the Library of Congress.

We would also build in the search engines and future tools that, as a collective resource, would connect us to the entire digital world.

All of this needs appropriate security and privacy assurances and ways to identify and acknowledge resources that can be trusted, relied on and somehow, miraculously, have all the copyright issues resolved.

CONCLUSION

The Web has brought librarians a new way to convey information. AACR2 and Dublin Core and other metadata schemas offer us tools to provide bibliographic control–that is, description and access–for those new materials and to link to the digital world. The metadata we provide needs to interoperate with other schemas to facilitate searching on the Web. The new twist is that the computer screen that displays the online catalog is also the device for viewing the actual digital objects and connecting to the entire digital world.

AUTHOR NOTE

Dr. Barbara B. Tillett is currently the Chief of the Cataloging Policy and Support Office (CPSO) at the Library of Congress. That division of about 50 people is responsible for various authoritative cataloging tools, including *LC Rule Interpretations*, *LC Classification* schedules, *LC Subject Headings*, and other cataloging documentation, such as the *Cataloging Service Bulletin*, *Descriptive Cataloging Manual*, *Subject Cataloging Manual*, etc. She is the Library of Congress representative on the Joint Steering Committee for Revision of the *Anglo-American Cataloguing Rules*. From February 2000-February 2001, she was the Interim/Acting Director for Electronic Resources for the Library of Congress, serving to coordinate various initiatives related to processing and accessing Aborn digital@ materials and providing bibliographic control for electronic resources. She also currently leads the Metadata Policy Group for the Library of Congress as part of the Library's digital strategic planning.

From 1997-2001 she was Director of the Integrated Library System (ILS) Program at the Library of Congress that successfully installed a new commercial Integrated Library System for the Library on time and on budget by October 1, 1999. For that accomplishment she received the Library's highest honor, the Distinguished Service Award, as well as the Arthur S. Flemming Award for outstanding federal service. Implementing the integrated library system (ILS) at the Library of Congress was the largest single automation project in the Library's history. It involved migrating 12 million bibliographic records, 5 million authority records, 20,000 patron records, 30,000 vendor records, over 55,000 open orders, and over 20 million holdings and item records from the Library's Alegacy@ stand-alone systems. The Library trained over 3,000 staff members, including 800 catalogers. The Library replaced over 2,000 workstations with new Pentium computers and installed a Sun E10000 server, all within an 18-month schedule with Y2K looming large.

Dr. Tillett's bachelor's degree is in mathematics (from Old Dominion University). Her master's and Ph.D. degrees are in library and information science, from the University of Hawaii and UCLA respectively. Her former positions have included bibliographic analyst and programmer for the Tsunami Document Retrieval System at the Hawaii Institute of Geophysics, University of Hawaii; Reference Librarian in science, technology, and medical reference at the Hamilton Library, University of Hawaii; OCLC System Coordinator for the University of California, San Diego; Director for Technical Services at the Scripps Institution of Oceanography Library; and head of the Catalog Department at the University of California, San Diego.

She has consulted on library automation, cataloging, authority control, and library technical operations, for example, serving as a consultant on conceptual modeling to the IFLA (International Federation of Library Associations) Study Group on the Functional Requirements of the Bibliographic Record, along with Tom Delsey, Elaine Svenonius, and Beth Dulabahn. Currently she chairs the IFLA Standing Committee Section on Cataloguing.

Her many publications have focused on cataloging theory and practice, authority control, bibliographic relationships, conceptual modeling, and library automation. Her dissertation on bibliographic relationships has been a source for conceptual designs of computer-based systems for bibliographic control.

Dr. Tillett has been active in the American Library Association throughout her 32 years as a librarian, including founding the Authority Control Interest Group in 1984. She was chair of the ALCTS Cataloging and Classification Section and now serves as the Library of Congress representative to the ALA Committee on Cataloging: Description and Access (CC:DA). She has served on several editorial and review boards for the major professional publications, including current work on the editorial board for *Cataloging & Classification Quarterly.*

REFERENCES

1. *Anglo-American Cataloguing Rules,* 2nd Edition, 2002 Revision.

2. Berners-Lee, Tim, James Hendler, and Ora Lassila. "The Semantic Web," *Scientific American* (May 2001), available on the Web http://www.scientificamerican.com/2001/0501issue/0501berners-lee.html.

Seriality:
What Have We Accomplished?
What's Next?

Jean Hirons

SUMMARY. Discusses the achievements and further goals of the revision of the *Anglo-American Cataloguing Rules* to accommodate various aspects of seriality. Focuses on the seriality of integrating resources (loose-leafs, Websites, databases) and explores their similarities to traditional serials as well as their differences, and the reasoning that led to the revised rules. Also analyzes decisions that have not been reached in the implementation of the rules at the time of this writing. Explains the decisions that will impact on both serials and integrating resources, and discusses the challenges that a new category of materials presents to the Program for Cooperative Cataloging's CONSER and BIBCO programs. Asks that readers consider how the seriality of these resources is being accommodated in their individual institutions. Highlights significant changes for serials and discusses the international harmonization effort and how it will benefit libraries in the United States of America.

KEYWORDS. AACR2R Chapter 12, serials, loose-leaf publications, Websites, integrating resources, continuing resources, international harmonization, ISBD(CR), cataloging

Jean Hirons is CONSER Coordinator, Serial Record Division, Library of Congress, 101 Independence Avenue, SE, Washington, DC 20540-4160 (E-mail: jhir@loc.gov). The article was transcribed by David C. Van Hoy, MIT.

[Haworth co-indexing entry note]: "Seriality: What Have We Accomplished? What's Next?" Hirons, Jean. Co-published simultaneously in *Cataloging & Classification Quarterly* (The Haworth Information Press, an imprint of The Haworth Press, Inc.) Vol. 36, No. 3/4, 2003, pp. 121-140; and: *Electronic Cataloging: AACR2 and Metadata for Serials and Monographs* (ed: Sheila S. Intner, Sally C. Tseng, and Mary Lynette Larsgaard) The Haworth Information Press, an imprint of The Haworth Press, Inc., 2003, pp. 121-140.

http://www.haworthpress.com/store/product.asp?sku=J104
10.1300/J104v36n03_10

INTRODUCTION

The seriality revision process had three basic goals: creation of descriptive cataloging rules for new types of resources; integration of the rules for seriality throughout the cataloging code; and harmonizing serial cataloging practices internationally.

The first goal was to create new rules in the *Anglo-American Cataloguing Rules* (AACR2) for new types of resources, such as loose-leaf services. Such services were not new and, because there were guidelines for loose-leafs, we were able to ignore the absence of specific rules for them in AACR2. However, when we started cataloging Websites and databases, many librarians objected to being instructed to catalog them as monographs, as was done with loose-leafs. Something else needed to be done with these new types of resources. This was the first–and probably most compelling–reason for initiating the rule revision process for serials.

The second goal was the integration of seriality throughout the cataloging code. Chapter 12 was never really thought sufficient in covering serials. Crystal Graham stated the case well in 1995, when she presented a paper analyzing AACR2 from the serials perspective.[1] She brought out many points that are covered in the revision of Chapter 12.

The third goal of this process was to harmonize cataloging practices internationally. Because serialists are now so dependent on the International Standard Serial Number (ISSN), and also on cataloging from national libraries and major university libraries in Europe and Asia, improved uniformity in our cataloging codes could permit more extensive sharing of catalog records from these varied sources.

Great progress toward these goals has been made in a relatively short period of time. Yet there is more to be done.

CREATING NEW RULES FOR NEW RESOURCES

It was a big challenge to fit loose-leafs, Websites, and databases into the monograph-serial dichotomy that is so firmly entrenched in libraries. For a long time, libraries have had their serial camps and monograph camps, but now, the division between them is starting to break down. Electronic resources, and the need to bring them into standard systems of bibliographic control, have served to bring the two camps together. However, major challenges remain to be addressed. At the Library of Congress, which has a serials cataloging division and multiple monograph cataloging divisions, where should these resources, having attributes of both types of publication, fit in? Other institutions have the same mono-graph-serial dichotomy and must address a similar challenge.

In the 2002 revision of AACR2, monographic items still are covered in Chapters 2 through 11. Included in this coverage will be stable works, issued in one or more parts, that exhibit no serial characteristics and are complete as first issued. Also included will be multiparts, publications issued in a succession of parts. These may or may not be complete when first issued, but they are still finite. Multiparts have not been moved into the revised Chapter 12, at least for now, but they are a topic for further discussion. Consideration will be given to the fact that, at least for a hard copy multipart, the updates, or parts, remain discrete, as issued. That is true for serials, too, of course. There are, in fact, many similarities between serials and multiparts.

AACR2's revised Chapter 12 is called "Continuing Resources." This is an umbrella term formulated in 1998 to cover two different types of ongoing publications: serials and what is now called "integrating resources." We wanted both types together because both exhibit characteristics of seriality. Both are ongoing and may change over time. But, because their forms of issuance differ, they require somewhat different cataloging rules. Serials, like multiparts, have updates, or parts, that remain discrete. Integrating resources, however, have updates that are integrated into the whole. One ends up with a single work, such as a loose-leaf, with no discrete parts, because the updates have been interfiled. For this reason it is not practical to catalog integrating resources using successive entry. They require different rules. The revised Chapter 12 acknowledges the differences by having rules specific to serials and rules specific to integrating resources.

The definitions in the revised appendix to AACR2 are as follows:[2]

Continuing resource. A bibliographic resource that has no predetermined conclusion.

Integrating resource. A bibliographic resource that is added to or changed by means of updates that do not remain discrete and are integrated into the whole. An integrating resource may be finite or continuing. Examples of integrating resources include updating loose-leafs and updating Websites.

Serial. A continuing resource issued in a succession of discrete parts, usually bearing numbering, that has no predetermined conclusion. Examples of serials include journals, magazines, electronic journals, continuing directories, annual reports, newspapers, and monographic series.

"Continuing resource" is a new concept that ties together resources that are issued with no predetermined conclusion, regardless of the form in which they are issued. "Integrating resource" is a new term for resources that are neither monographs nor serials. Crystal Graham, in her earlier work, called these "bibliographic hermaphrodites!"[3] Integrating resource, exemplified by loose-leafs and updating Websites, was selected to label this new concept. Because the term describes only the form of issuance, an integrating resource can be either finite or continuing. You could have, for example, a Website for a political campaign that eventually comes to an end.

The new definition of serial went through many iterations, and in the end was changed far less than it might have been. In the new definition, the word "discrete" has been added as has the word "usually." The three basic criteria for seriality are still present, but they have been changed and softened. The word "discrete" was added to accommodate numbered articles in an electronic journal that has no issues. "Usually bearing numbering" makes it possible for unnumbered series to be considered serials, primarily for purposes of entry and title changes. This doesn't open the serial door to every kind of unnumbered publication, however. Numbering is still a key characteristic of serials. The final part of the definition, "has no predetermined conclusion," was taken from ISSN, and seems softer and easier to apply that the old "is intended to continue indefinitely."

In defining "serial" there were other types of publications to include, such as publications that look like serials but are reports from a limited duration event. First we tried to fit them into the new definition. But it just didn't work. It seemed impossible to find definitions that would accommodate these added varieties of resources while maintaining clear distinctions between what was to be treated as a serial and what was to be treated as a multipart monograph. Instead, the scope of Chapter 12 was broadened in specific ways. The scope rule, 12.0A, was written to specify that certain other types of resources can be cataloged with the rules in Chapter 12. While they cannot technically be called continuing resources, they can be cataloged according to the rules for serials and integrating resources.

One category of this sort is resources that exhibit characteristics of serials, such as successive issues, numbering, and frequency, but that are finite in nature. Examples would be the newsletters of an event or the quarterly technical reports of a project. They look like serials, act like serials, librarians want to check them in like serials, but they are not going to continue indefinitely. A second category is "reprints of serials." These have been cataloged as serials according to a Library of Congress Rule Interpretation in order to keep all versions of a serial together, even if the reprint is issued as a finite number of bound volumes. The third and last category specified for inclusion is "finite integrating resources." We recognize that an integrating resource can be finite or continuing, but it can be difficult to make that determination, and it was believed not worth trying to force the distinction. There are no differences in the cataloging of the two types, and there are no differences in the MARC coding of them. So, rules for all integrating resources are contained in Chapter 12.

Describing integrating resources was the second major challenge. Latest entry cataloging conventions have been applied to loose-leafs and to updating databases and websites. Would applying latest entry to one category of continuing resources suggest it be applied to all? Successive entry (separate records for each major change) is the keystone of ISSN and making such a major change to serials cataloging practice seemed unwise. At one point alternatives, such as "integrating entry," which was a combination of both, were considered. In the end, the decision was to stay with successive entry for serials and latest entry for integrating resources, which is the current practice. Description of an integrating resource will be based on its latest iteration. (The word "iteration" is being used here because we are referring to the integrating resource as viewed in its entirety, not to its latest issue, as for a serial.) Earlier descriptive information will be carried within notes. Most changes affecting an integrating resource will be recorded in a single record describing the entire existence of the resource. Changes in edition (area 2) may require a new record. This practice will apply to all integrating resources.

With the AACR2 decisions made for integrating resources it was time to address the related MARC coding questions. In June 2001, the Committee on Representation of Machine-Readable Bibliographic Instruction (MARBI) approved a proposal for a new bibliographic level code "i" (for "integrating resource"). It will be used in conjunction with the same fixed field (008) used in describing serials. Using the same fixed field recognizes the serial aspects of these resources. For example, like serials, integrating resources have frequency, publication status, and beginning and ending dates of publication–all characteristics that can be recorded in a 008 field. Some new values applicable specifically to integrating resources have been added to the MARC 21 format. A new frequency code has been defined to indicate a title is updated continually. A new code has been added to the Successive/Latest Entry fixed field to designate "integrated entry," which distinguishes records created for integrating resources under current rules from the old serial latest entry records created under prior rules. The bad news, of course, is that there is no telling when this coding will be implemented. Until it is, we continue coding integrating resources as "m" (for monograph). No interim practice permits using code "s" (for serial).

With integrating resource defined in AACR2 and coded in MARC 21, the difficult task of deciding more precisely what resources are included in the definition had to be faced. The issue was discussed at the Library of Congress for some time. We settled on three features that define an integrating resource. The first and most important feature is that only a single title is used for the resource at any one time, primarily because it has only a single chief source of information at any one time. If the title of the resource changes, the new title appears at the same time that the old title disappears. The old title might still be mentioned somewhere at the site in a history note or an "about" file, but the title on the chief source simply changes over to the new title. That differs from a serial, which has extant issues or parts still carrying the old title. The second feature defining an integrating resource is that new material, or updates, do not remain discrete as issues or parts, but are interfiled or absorbed into the resource. The third is that it is a resource intended for updating, whether the updating is intended to be continual or for a finite period of time.

It might be helpful to look at some examples. The first example, *Alcohol Industry & Policy Database*,[4] is an online database intended to be updated monthly (see Figure 1). The chief source shows a single title, a search interface, and a statement about the updates, but no evidence that updates exist separately from the resource itself. This is a good example of an updating database, a type of resource we must now catalog as a monograph.

The second example, *bizjournals.com*,[5] is a Website for a company that publishes several local business newspapers (see Figure 2). On their site they have local breaking news, various articles, a lot of clearly labeled information on how to purchase their newspapers and other items, and so on. The site is intended to be updated, and is, in fact, updated frequently, as is evident from the prominent date and time stamp on the home page. The site has only one title. Although this title may appear on any number of screens at the Website, the chief source shows only the single title. If the site's owners should decide on a title change, that single title is sure to be changed on the chief source and all the other screens where it appears. Many Websites are set up like this one and al-

FIGURE 1. Alcohol Industry & Policy Database

The Marin Institute
for the Prevention of Alcohol and Other Drug Problems

24 Belvedere Street, San Rafael, CA 94901 USA (415) 456-5692 FAX (415) 456-0491

Alcohol Industry & Policy Database

As part of our goal to hold accountable those who profit from harmful conditions, the Marin Institute acts as a watchdog of alcohol marketing practices. What distinguishes our approach to the prevention of alcohol-related problems is that instead of focusing on individual risk factors, we concentrate on the environments that support and glamorize alcohol use. The alcohol beverage industry, which spends one billion dollars annually to advertise its products and lobbies heavily for favorable public policy, is a large component of our social and political environment.

This database contains citations and brief abstracts for over thirteen thousand articles and news stories about the alcohol beverage industry, alcohol policy, and prevention efforts. The time period covered is 1991 to the present; the Web version is updated monthly. Sources include major newspaper and business journals, as well as journals from the fields of prevention, advertising, and the beverage industry. The database is indexed using subject headings from the *Marin Institute Thesaurus*.

Searching Tip: If you are having trouble finding citations searching the subject or company fields, click on the Word Wheel button to choose from a list of terms; if this is unsuccessful, try searching the keyword field. For more help in formulating searches, click on the Help button below.

KEYWORDS

SUBJECT HEADINGS (This field uses a controlled vocabulary)

COMPANY NAME

PUBLICATION DATE

AUTHOR

most always the intention is to keep them up-to-date. After consideration of all these factors, a likely conclusion is that many Websites can be categorized as integrating resources.

On the other hand, one cannot assume that because something is posted at a Website it is an integrating resource or a serial. The following example, *Background Notes: Bangladesh*,[6] is a monograph (see Figure 3). It is a report that happens to be available online, but there is no intention to update it. Clearly printed in its top paragraph is the phrase "this site is not updated."

Still, questions remain as to what is and is not to be considered an integrating resource. What is the difference between an integrating resource and a collection? Collections, such as archival collections, may continue to be augmented. One difference is that an integrating resource is a single published title to which material is added, whereas a collection is likely to be comprised of a variety of items, not all of them necessarily published.

FIGURE 2. Bizjournals.com

FIGURE 3. Background Notes: Bangladesh

The State Department web site below is a permanent electronic archive of information released prior to January 20, 2001. Please see www.state.gov for material released since President George W. Bush took office on that date. This site is not updated so external links may no longer function. Contact us with any questions about finding information.

NOTE: External links to other Internet sites should not be construed as an endorsement of the views contained therein.

U.S. Department of State, March 2000
Bureau of South Asian Affairs

Background Notes:
Bangladesh

U.S. Relations	Official Name: People's Republic of Bangladesh
History	PROFILE Geography
Economy	Area: 143,998 sq. km. (55,813 sq. mi.), about the size of Wisconsin

Could a cumulative CD-ROM be an integrating resource? With these, the outdated CD is discarded when a new one arrives, so a library has only one item with the one title at any time. CD-ROMs are discrete and a library could keep the outdated ones if they wished. A succession of CD-ROMs carrying the same title (or carrying a succession of title changes) could be retained.

Might non-textual resources be considered integrating? Consider a set of medical slides, where a library might receive a monthly update containing new and replacement slides, much like a loose-leaf. What about a cartographic Website with weather maps that are constantly being updated? Are there sound recording resources that might be considered integrating resources–perhaps a continually updated database of birdcalls?

These and other questions must be considered. A working group at the Library of Congress is looking at many of them and, eventually, will issue a Library of Congress Rule Interpretation. This working group will consult with OnLine Audiovisual Catalogers (OLAC, the specialized association that works with audiovisual and electronic resource material), and will also take up questions with members of the Program for Cooperative Cataloging (CONSER and BIBCO). The working group will do a great deal of consulting and provide opportunities for comments. The rule interpretation, when issued, will serve as the basis for all the documentation on integrating resources that follows.

IMPLEMENTATION ISSUES

Beyond the basic questions about what should be considered an integrating resource are complex implementation issues. What will catalogers do if the form of issuance of an item changes from serial to integrating, or if the form fluctuates between the two? Will new records be required for each change of form or will it be possible to make changes to a single record? This is a serious issue for the Library of Congress because there are different record distribution streams for different types of records. What policies will apply to the linking of records? Thinking beyond the linking of serial records, what about linking serials to integrating resources? If such links are made between records, record maintenance will become more time-consuming and complex. Whenever there is a change to the title of the integrating resource, that title will also have to be revised in the notes on any records linked to that integrating resource. Shall uniform titles be assigned to records for integrating resources, as is done for serials? If they are, then what is to be done when the title changes on the integrating resource? Similarly, under what circumstances would the qualifier used in the uniform title of an integrating resource be changed? If there were a name change for a corporate body used in the qualifier, would the uniform title be revised accordingly? What about other changes affecting qualifying terms? A number of fundamental guidelines must be established.

Yet another collection of questions in need of decisions relates to the effects on cooperative cataloging programs, CONSER and BIBCO. With CONSER responsible for serial records and BIBCO responsible for monograph records, where do integrating resource records fit in? A Program for Cooperative Cataloging Task Group on Implementation of Integrating Resources has been established to study these related questions and problems. It is likely that both CONSER and BIBCO catalogers will be able to establish and maintain records for integrating resources. Ideally, the broadest possible grouping of catalogers would be able to maintain records for integrating resources in a network database such as OCLC's.

Maintenance for the records of integrating resources is a complex issue. CONSER catalogers routinely and regularly update a serial record in OCLC so that the record reflects the important bibliographic details of an entire work over its known lifetime. The record does not just describe the first or earliest available issue of a serial. But such record maintenance has not been as critical to BIBCO. Will BIBCO catalogers be able to adopt record maintenance as standard practice? ·

For the Library of Congress especially, record distribution questions need to be addressed. At present, CONSER serial records are created and maintained solely on OCLC. CONSER records are then distributed to RLIN and other recipients, which is where many libraries pick up those records. The Library of Congress does not distribute BIBCO records added to the OCLC or RLIN network databases. No records created for integrating resources to this point have been distributed. But, what should be done with records for integrating resources once these changes are implemented? Such questions must be decided by the Policy Committee of the Program for Cooperative Cataloging.

After decisions have been made, the tasks of writing documentation and training catalogers follow. Documentation will definitely be developed for the *CONSER Cataloging Manual* and for the *BIBCO Participants' Manual,* but it is also likely to be available elsewhere via the World Wide Web.

What challenges might face libraries locally, in their own systems? For online catalogs there may be ramifications for searching, labeling, and display. There may be acquisitions issues for those using integrated library systems that combine acquisitions with other systems. Will cataloging responsibilities, which so often follow the traditional monograph-serial dichotomy, be changed by the introduction of integrating resources as a third category? Is it possible a library could follow metadata standards other than AACR for some materials, particularly for online resources?

SERIALITY: CHANGES TO AACR2 AND MARC 21

An important change involves Rule 12.0B1, Chief Source of Information. Because two decisions must be made when describing a serial (which issue will serve as the basis of the description and from where in that issue the title will come), the rule was split in two. Rule 12.0B1 will now cover the basis for the description, and 12.0B2 will cover the choice of chief source. Prescribed sources (the chief source and other approved places in addition to it) are further described in 12.0B3.

The description of serials will still be based on the earliest piece. A change back to latest entry was considered, but found to be unworkable. Integrating resources will be described from the latest iteration. The choice of chief source will not change for printed serials. For CD-ROMs, however, there is a change of preference to the carrier or its labels, because CD-ROM serials must be handled by serials check-in staff and, therefore, it is preferable to base their description on an eye-readable source. This rule will not be included in Chapter 9, because there is no change for monographic CD-ROMs, but will be located in Chapter 12 instead. The preferred basis for the description of remote electronic serials will be the first issue or part, rather than a home page. One reason for this selection is that a title appearing on the first issue is less likely to be changed–and changed retrospectively on each issue–than is a title appearing on a serial's home page.

Some changes that reflect seriality are small and some will not seem new to those who have been following the Library of Congress Rule Interpretations or using the *CONSER Cataloging Manual*. A number of specific practices that had been put into practice in CONSER now appear in the rules themselves, for example, the ability to correct mistakes in the title proper rather than recording an error as it appears on the issue being described, and permission to ignore phrases such as "Welcome to" when they precede the main title.

Much work went into drafting several changes related to serial designations. One of the best made by the Joint Steering Committee, in April

2001, was renaming the "Numeric and/or Alphabetic, Chronological, or Other Designation Area" to "Numbering Area"! (Catalogers called it "the 362" for lack of a better term.) The exact transcription of punctuation from the issue is no longer required, for example, one can replace a dash appearing in multiple dates with a slash to achieve greater clarity (e.g., "2000/2001-2003/2004" rather than "2000-2001-2003-2004"). Broader permission is granted to supply dates as well as numbers when the first issue lacks them. In a move harmonizing with the ISSN guidelines, a change in numbering back to "volume 1," for example, will be accounted for within an existing record by supplying the term "new series." It is not necessary to close an existing record and initiate a new one merely because numbering restarts.

To clarify a rule that has been open to different interpretations, there are specific instructions not to record date(s) of publication when the first and/or last issues are not in hand. Also new, though, is an option that allows the presumed date(s) to be recorded in brackets, a current practice of the National Library of Canada.

Rules for notes have been greatly expanded, one reason being that instructions had to be specified for both serials and integrating resources. Because their descriptions are based on different issues/iterations, their notes differ accordingly, with notes for serials referring to later issues, and notes for integrating resources referring to earlier iterations. While the rules for notes for continuing resources will be more complex, they will also be more complete. One specific new rule specifies that linking notes are applicable to integrating resources as well as serials. Also, for serials only, the "latest issue consulted" information that was recorded only as local information (the MARC 936 field in CONSER records on OCLC) will now be specified by the rules themselves as data to be recorded in conjunction with the "description based on" note. This move satisfies one of the original goals of the seriality process, which was to recognize that the record was intended to describe the entire work–that is, the entire serial–not just its first or earliest available issue.

The major MARC change related to seriality is the introduction of multiple 260 fields (Publication, distribution, etc.). Proposal 2001-04, approved by the Committee on Machine-Readable Bibliographic Information (MARBI) in June 2001, establishes repeatable 260 fields. In current records, latest publisher information is buried in the note fields (500). Yet this information is more valuable to acquisitions staff and other users than publisher information from the earliest issue. While earliest publisher information is needed for record matching, latest publisher information is needed for ordering, claiming, and other acquisitions-related tasks. New first indicator values in the 260 field will serve to distinguish the various types of publisher information. A blank in the first indicator position will continue to designate earliest publisher data, first indicator value "3" will be used to designate latest publisher data, and value "2" will be used for all intervening publishers. Additionally, the new subfield "3" in the 260 field will be used to record date or numbering information that is currently included in free text format in the notes (500 field).

Following is a hypothetical example of multiple 260 fields in a serial record:

```
260    $a Boston, MA : $b Houghton Mifflin, $c 1987-2003.
260 2  $3 1990-1999 $a Boston, MA : $b Harcourt
260 3  $3 2000-2003 $a Boston, MA : $b Harvard University Press
```

This example is for a serial that is no longer published. Beginning and ending dates of publication are kept together in the $c of the first 260 field. The more recent dates, carried in $3s, are dates related to chronology–the issue information that until this point was carried in the 500 fields. For output, as in catalog displays, the 260 fields might be combined into a single note, looking much like the former 500 field note. But for a brief display, in the acquisitions module of an integrated library system, for example, the output might be restricted to the 260 $3 when present, or restricted to the 260 field with a blank first indicator when there is no 260 $3 in the record.

A hypothetical example of multiple 260 fields in an integrating resource record would look as follows:

```
260    $3 1999-<2001?> $a Cambridge, MA : $b MIT Press
260 3  $3 <2001?>-2002 $a Cambridge, MA : $b Harvard University Press, $c 1999-2002.
```

This example is for an integrating resource that is no longer published. Beginning and ending dates of publication are still kept together in the $c, but in this case the $c is part of the latest publisher information, as specified by the new cataloging rules. Because it was not possible to change the meaning of the indicator values between serials and integrating resources, changing where the single $c appeared was seen as the appropriate approach. For both types of publications the 260 field carrying a "3" in the first indicator position contains the most recent publication information.

PENDING ISSUES

These are not all of the changes to AACR2 and to MARC 21 related to seriality, but they are the most significant. Some seriality-related issues have not yet been dealt with fully. Multiparts, for example, which behave much like serials, but are finite, are not covered in Chapter 12, so they have not been touched by these changes. Judy Kuhagen, from the Library of Congress Cataloging Policy and Support Office, has written a complete review of the status of multipart publications in AACR2. The Joint Steering Committee is expected to review this work. Also, non-textual serials are not addressed directly in the other chapters of AACR2; their monographic orientation remains.

A recommendation was made that Part I of AACR2 be reorganized by area of description. That approach was thought to be a better way to give non-textual seriality better coverage. Multipart publications also might fit better into a Part I reorganized in that manner. But such a major reorganization of the rules has not happened yet, and may not be such a good idea.

INTERNATIONAL HARMONIZATION

A key reason that rule harmonization is important relates to the International Standard Serial Number (ISSN). The ISSN has become one of the most useful tools for managing serial collections because of its use in ordering and maintenance of subscriptions, and because of the hooks to library holdings features in some electronic reference tools. But when a one-to-one correspondence between an ISSN and bibliographic record does not exist, ISSN's usefulness is diminished. Working toward more one-to-one relationships between ISSNs and bibliographic records was seen as a valuable objective. This would also allow greater record sharing and exchange between ISSN catalogers and AACR catalogers.

Similarly, more widespread exchange of records between AACR and non-AACR catalogers would be possible if there were greater harmonization in the rules they follow. There is certainly increased interest in participation in cooperative cataloging programs. CONSER has become more international in the last year, with additions to its membership for the National Library of Wales and the Hong Kong University of Science and Technology. The more correspondence there is between different records for a title, the more sharing can occur in creating and maintaining those records. With smaller cataloging staffs (as at the Library of Congress), fewer catalogers proficient in non-English languages, and the acquisition of more materials in lesser-known languages, the more desirable is the ability to seek out and utilize other bibliographic records, such as those from other national catalogs, in whatever format, to aid in the creation of one's own record.

Three groups are participating in the harmonization efforts: the Joint Steering Committee (for AACR), with Ann Huthwaite, Chair of the Committee, leading the group; the ISBD(S) Working Group, with Ingrid Parent chairing the group; and the ISSN Manual Revision Committee, with Françoise Pellé of the ISSN Centre in Paris chairing that group.

The *International Standard Bibliographic Description (Serials)* (ISBD(S)), which actually forms the basis for AACR, provides the cataloging rules used in many of the countries where AACR is not used. It is revised only irregularly, but is now undergoing major revision for the first time in many years. The draft revision, available at this writing, was to be finalized during the 2001 IFLA meeting in Boston. Procedures for ISSN cataloging are also undergoing revision.

Representatives from the three groups met at the Library of Congress in November 2000 for a "Meeting of Experts." Prior to that meeting, key issues were identified for discussion. Some differences, such as rules applicable to "other title information," were not considered key issues because they do not affect decisions about the need for a new record. Ultimately, the objective is to have everyone, regardless of the cataloging rules being followed, make the same decision about the need for a new serial record.

Perhaps the most basic determination made prior to the meeting related to what materials or resources were to be encompassed by the discussions. "Continuing resources," which has become a broadly accepted concept, was agreed upon as the scope of resources under discussion. The revised version of ISBD(S) will be known as ISBD(CR), reflecting its newly established scope. The full name will be *International Standard Bibliographic Description (Serials and Other Continuing Resources)*. Continuing resources will become the scope for the ISSN as well. Soon ISSNs will be assigned not just to serials but also to continuing resources, though probably not to finite integrating resources. The experts also discussed and agreed on definitions of the terms "serial," "integrating resource," and "continuing resource."

It was agreed that rules for title transcription were a key to harmonization in title change decisions. Only if there is agreement on the transcription of the title in the first place can there be agreement subsequently on whether that title has changed. AACR2's rules for transcription of a full title and its initialism has had one exception to the practice of selecting the full title as the title proper and the initialism as other title information. By removing that exception from AACR2, the issue was resolved.

Harmonizing the rules for title changes, an important agenda issue, was more difficult. Conceptually, the objective was to be able to recognize when there was a title change that everyone could agree was significant, as opposed to a change so insignificant it might not even be noticed. A title change requiring a new record should be prompted by a deliberate change in the work itself, not caused unintentionally by some innocent act of the publisher. And, because people other than catalogers (such as acquisitions and check-in staff) must also be able to recognize possible title changes, the rules must be fairly straightforward. Any new rules developed for title changes have to be understandable to a broad range of individuals, successful in reducing the number of new records created unintentionally, and agreed upon internationally so that all create a new record at the same point.

It was decided that the ISBD concept of major and minor title changes would be introduced into AACR. Three title variation situations new to AACR2 were agreed upon as minor title changes. First, it was agreed that the addition or deletion of words anywhere in the title that represent the type of publication, such as "journal," "magazine," and "series," are minor variations, but not words indicating frequency, such as "monthly" and "annual." The change from *C* to *C Magazine* would be a minor title change, as would the change from *Bowling Journal* to *Bowling*. But the change from *The Atlantic* to *Atlantic Monthly* would still be considered a major title change. Excluding frequency words was seen as necessary to keep the rules from becoming so loose that a change from *Annual Report* to *Quarterly Bulletin* would not be considered a major change! It was agreed that a change in frequency was more likely to indicate a real change in the publication. Another exclusion was cases where the word is changed, rather than added or deleted. Again, it was decided that where a word is changed, as when a title goes from *Wilson Review* to *Wilson Bulletin*, it was likely to be a real change in the publication. In the end, the rule was limited to just additions and deletions of words indicating type of publication.

Second, a difference involving the name of the same corporate body and elements of its hierarchy or their grammatical connection anywhere in the title was agreed to be a minor variation. This referred to the addition, deletion, or rearrangement of the name of the same corporate body or the substitution of a variant form of the name of the body anywhere in the title. For example, a change from *Bulletin of the U.S. Geological Survey* to *Geological Survey Bulletin* would be considered a minor title change. A subsequent change from *Geological Survey Bulletin* to *USGS Bulletin* would likewise be considered minor. However, when the name of the corporate body truly changes and prompts a new name authority record, the new title must be considered a major title change.

Third, the addition to, deletion from, or change in the order of words in a list anywhere in a title, provided there is no significant change in the subject matter, is not to be considered a major change. This does not refer to the situation where *Physics and Chemistry Bulletin* changes to *Physics Bulletin*. Two items given in a title in that manner do not constitute a list. A title containing a series of city, country, chemical, animal, or other topical names, where the names are likely to come and go, and get rearranged, is what this rule is intended to cover. A hypothetical example might be a change from *Touring Boston, Lexington, Concord, Gloucester, and Newburyport* to *Touring Boston, Lexington, and Concord, Gloucester and Newburyport, New Bedford and Cape Cod*. A rule interpretation, including several examples, will probably be necessary to clarify specifically when to apply the rule.

Some decisions for implementing these new title change rules are set already. The rules will apply prospectively, not retrospectively. Merging existing records will not be an option, primarily because, for libraries with holdings and check-in records attached to the bibliographic records, merging causes significant aggravation. Libraries were cautioned not to apply the rules before the publication of AACR2 2002 (which has since happened) because a major goal in the seriality process was harmonization; therefore, it was vital that implementation be timed to coincide with implementation by the ISSN centers.

While title change rules turned out to be the major harmonization decisions to come out of the Meeting of Experts, there were other decisions as well. As mentioned earlier, there was agreement that a numbering change, or a restart in numbering, would not require a new bibliographic record. And there was an agreement to disagree on whether to establish a successive entry or latest entry policy for integrating resource records. While ISBD(CR) and AACR will follow a latest entry policy, the ISSN will use successive entry for all continuing resources. There is hope that these two different practices will not cause significant problems for bibliographic utility databases, but the specifics for dealing with this challenge must still be worked out.

UNRESOLVED ISSUES

Some harmonization issues remain unresolved. Rules for transcription of titles that include both common titles and part titles, or series and subseries, remain a challenge. A special expert working group will be set up to discuss this issue further.

Transliteration of titles in non-Roman alphabets is an issue that seems unresolvable, because many different transliteration schemes are in use. It may be that this issue can be resolved only by the use of vernacular scripts rather than transliteration.

A major topic tossed around in a number of serials-related meetings for the past few years is what has been called the "International Standard Serial Title" (ISST). Conceived as a replacement for the key title and the uniform title in most cases–perhaps not all–it has been envisioned as the entry that could serve as a universal benchmark in making title change decisions. Such a universal benchmark would maximize the use of the ISSN in library operations, because it helps achieve one-to-one correspondence between an ISSN and a single bibliographic record.

Several major challenges must be addressed before agreement on an ISST can be reached. While significant steps have been made toward harmonization in recording titles, differences still exist for establishing a uniform main entry. AACR uses corporate main entry for many serials; ISBD does not. For uniform titles, AACR uses corporate body in its authoritative form for a qualifier; ISSN and ISBD(CR) use corporate body in the form in which it appears on the piece. Would ISSTs be assigned to monographic series? Would ISSTs be assigned to integrating resources? Would monograph catalogers, as well as serials catalogers, determine ISSTs?

How would a procedure be set up to establish, on an international basis, the ISST for a title? Could the ISSN database be extended to serve as a central serial title authority file? In order to establish an international standard serial title that would never change, a cataloger would have to have access not just to his or her own network or utility (such as OCLC or RLIN), but to the international database serving as repository for all ISSTs. Only a central database could assure that a particular ISST was indeed unique. Is it possible to set up an automatic ISST approval system, with catalogers utilizing application forms available at the ISSN Website?

This scenario, in all of its variations, would require internationally approved procedures and sophisticated data networking. An initial step in what could be a long process might be an analysis of potential costs and benefits. Is there sufficient benefit to justify the costs? Could bibliographic differences be resolved or, at least, not hinder the effort? Is the system technically feasible? Assuming sufficient promise can be demonstrated, a pilot project should probably be conducted. This is a major endeavor, sure to take some time; but it is not merely a dream. An ISST Working Group now exists, coordinated by Françoise Pellé, the ISSN Director. In addition to myself, the other members of the working group are Renate Gömpel of the Deutsche Bibliothek, Ingrid Parent of the National Library of Canada, Alain Roucolle from the ISSN Centre, and Regina Reynolds from the United States ISSN Center at the Library of Congress.

CONCLUSION

One can only wonder what new challenges await serials catalogers in the more distant future that will demand attention when those just described are successfully resolved. Perhaps the only thing we can be sure of is that we cannot foresee the last of them.

AUTHOR NOTE

Jean Hirons is a native of Massachusetts, having been born in Boston, and worked her first years as a librarian at Southeastern Massachusetts University, now the University of Massachusetts, Dartmouth. She earned her MLS at the University of Rhode Island and subsequently moved to the Washington, DC area where she worked at the Government Printing Office as a serials specialist and supervisor. In 1983 she moved to the Library of Congress, taking on a dual job of forming a part time minimal level cataloging section and assisting the CONSER Coordinator. During that time she created the CONSER Editing Guide and CONSER Cataloging Manual. In 1997 she became CONSER Coordinator after serving in an acting capacity for four years. As such, she has been involved with all of the major cataloging issues from format integration to electronic serials. In 1997, she and Crystal Graham co-authored the paper *Issues Related to Seriality*, which they presented at the International Conference on the Principles and Future Direction of AACR. The Joint Steering Committee on the Revision of AACR subsequently charged her with creating rule revision proposals in support of the recommendations in the Hirons/Graham paper, the topic she discusses in this paper.

In addition, Ms. Hirons is the founder of the Serials Cataloging Cooperative Training Program, which she formed with her colleagues in the serials community in order to meet the growing need for quality serials instruction. The program and the distributed model upon which it is based have proven to be highly successful and will be expanded to other areas of cataloging. She is the recipient of the 1996 Bowker/Ulrich's Serials Librarianship award for her contributions to documentation, training, and leadership in the serials cataloging arena. When she isn't revising cataloging codes, Ms. Hirons is a pastel painter and pianist.

REFERENCES

1. Jean Hirons and Crystal Graham. "Issues Related to Seriality," in *International Conference on the Principles and Future Development of AACR: The Principles and Future of AACR.* Jean Weihs, ed. (Chicago: American Library Association, 1998), p. 180-213.

2. *Anglo-American Cataloguing Rules*, 2nd ed., 2002 revision (Ottawa: Canadian Library Association, 2002), p. Appendix D-2, D-4.

3. Crystal Graham and Rebecca Ringler, "Hermaphrodites and Herrings," *Serials Review*, 22, no. 1 (Spring 1996): p. 73-77.

4. Available at http://marin.andornot.com/.

5. Available at http://bizjournals.bcentral.com/.

6. Available at http://www.state.gov/www/background_notes/bangladesh_0003_bgn.html.

MARC and Mark-Up

Erik Jul

SUMMARY. Discusses the development and implications of electronic resource description systems, including the familiar library standard, the
MARC Format, and the newly developing Resource Description Format
(RDF), as well as other non-library markup languages such as XML, HTML,
SGML, etc. Explains the differences between content and container, and the
kinds of rules needed for describing each. Closes by outlining clearly why it is
important for librarians to reach out beyond the library community and partic-
ipate in the development of metadata standards. *[Article copies available for a
fee from The Haworth Document Delivery Service: 1-800-HAWORTH. E-mail address: <docdelivery@haworthpress.com> Website: <http://www.HaworthPress.com>
© 2003 by The Haworth Press, Inc. All rights reserved.]*

KEYWORDS. MARC, XML, HTML, mark-up languages, metadata
standards, content, container, encoding schema

INTRODUCTION

In the early 1990s, OCLC's Office of Research conducted a project
studying the suitability of applying the *Anglo-American Cataloguing
Rules* (AACR2) and MARC format to the emerging world of electronic

Erik Jul was formerly Executive Director, OCLC Institute, OCLC Online Computer Library Center, Inc., 6565 Frantz Road, Dublin, OH 43017-5308.

[Haworth co-indexing entry note]: "MARC and Mark-Up." Jul, Erik. Co-published simultaneously in *Cataloging & Classification Quarterly* (The Haworth Information Press, an imprint of The Haworth Press, Inc.) Vol.
36, No. 3/4, 2003, pp. 141-153; and: *Electronic Cataloging: AACR2 and Metadata for Serials and Monographs*
(ed: Sheila S. Intner, Sally C. Tseng, and Mary Lynette Larsgaard) The Haworth Information Press, an imprint
of The Haworth Press, Inc., 2003, pp. 141-153. Single or multiple copies of this article are available for a fee
from The Haworth Document Delivery Service [1-800-HAWORTH, 9:00 a.m. - 5:00 p.m. (EST). E-mail address: docdelivery@haworthpress.com].

10.1300/J104v36n03_11 *141*

resources–long before the World Wide Web became a reality. A peer led me proudly to a computer with a blank screen and a cursor blinking on the monitor, and said, "There it is!" At that point, the network consisted mainly of telnet and ftp. There was a time during the early days of the Web when OCLC could easily run a search on every Website and its directories. I can remember when there were just a little more than a thousand Websites. Now, the Web is considerably larger and the logical possibilities for dealing with it are three: apply AACR2 to its resources as is; add to AACR2 to make it more suitable; or use something other than AACR2.

At this juncture, we should note that none of the non-library metadata standards specifies form of entry. It is up to us, the library community, to step forward with instructions that make metadata usable, meaningful, and retrievable. But, for us to understand what is going on with non-library metadata standards, we need to separate the rules from both the content and the container of the resource being described–a concept with which librarians have become familiar in recent years. In this presentation, I'll talk about the container–not the rules or the content.

RESOURCE DESCRIPTION

One can achieve structure in resource descriptions in many ways, including alternative ways that differ from our highly structured world of AACR2 and MARC. We need to understand the problem of resource description as viewed through the eyes of other communities, ask questions, and then determine our course of action. It is certainly preferable that we who have worked for so long on describing resources define the course of resource description, instead of being forced into a path by the external world, which generally does not have our background and experience in working with information. But to be successful in this course, we need to understand that external world and the non-library communities within it.

Not so many years ago at a meeting, I said, "Who in this audience has identified, selected and cataloged at least one Web resource, using AACR2 and MARC?" In response, perhaps two persons raised their hands. When I ask that question at this Metadata Institute, I would expect a majority of the participants to respond. People in this audience have done exactly that work. We needed to see if it worked or what adjustments needed to be made to make it work, and we have done just that in programs such as INTERCAT (Internet Cataloging Project) and CORC (Cooperative Online Resource Catalog).

Structured information can come in a variety of forms. The most common forms seen in libraries are bibliographic records and tagged fields in a markup language. The Library of Congress's Cataloging-in-Publication data is an example of resource description that actually appears in the item (see Figure 1).

The way a resource description looks to computer software is quite different from how it looks to human eyes. It has a James-Joyce-Ulysses look of being one long sentence punctuated by delimiters–which might appear as carats (^) (see Figure 2).

The degree to which a tagged MARC record is understandable plummets when it is viewed by anyone other than a cataloger, for example, slide a tagged MARC record under the nose of the person at a hotel checkout and see how much more quickly they will process your paperwork! Catalogers have a set of rules in mind when they look at tagged records. The average person does not know these rules even though many people are accustomed to seeing cataloging in standard catalog card format; but, even for a card, they are unlikely to recognize everything. For example, take the Arabic and roman numerals used, respectively, to list subjects and added entries. Librarians know the difference, but most laypersons do not. Catalog card displays are meaningful to us because of their implicit structure, with which we have become familiar over a great many years.

What happens when we move our rules into a machine environment? The MARC record originally was created and defined to perform certain functions in a mainframe computer environment, and to enable printing of catalog cards. As a communications format it has certain limitations

FIGURE 1. Cataloging-in-Publication

Library of Congress Cataloging-in-Publication Data

OCLC 1967-1997 : thirty years of furthering access to the world's information / K. Wayne Smith, editor.
    p. cm.
    "Co-published simultaneously as Journal of library administration, volume 25, numbers 2/3 and 4, 1998."
    Includes bibliographical references (p.) and index.
    ISBN 0-7890-0536-0 (hardcover : alk. paper). – ISBN 0-7890-0542-5 (pbk. : alk. paper)
    1. OCLC–History. 2. Library information networks–History. 3. Library information networks–United States–History. I. Smith, K. Wayne. II. Journal of library administration.
Z674.82.015016 1998
021.6′5′09–dc21
                                    98-15155
                                          CIP

FIGURE 2. MARC-Tagged Cataloging

```
01041cam  2200265 a 45000010020000000030004000200_0
50017000240080041000410100024000820200025001060200
04400131040001800175050002400193082001800217100003
20023524500870026724600360035425000120039026000370
040230000290043950000420046852002200051065000033007
30650001200763^###89048230#/AC/r91^DLC^19911106082
810.9^891101s1990####maua###j######000#0#eng##^##$
a###89048230#/AC/r91^##$a0316107514 :$c$12.95^##$a
0316107506 (pbk.) :$c$5.95 ($6.95 Can.)^##$aDLC$cD
LC$dDLC^00$aGV943.25$b.B74 1990^00$a796.334/2$220^
10$aBrenner, Richard J.,$d1941-^10$aMake the team.
$pSoccer :$ba heads up guide to super soccer! /$cR
ichard J. Brenner.^30$aHeads up guide to super soc
cer.^##$a1st ed.^##$aBoston :$bLittle, Brown,$cc19
90.^##$a127 p. :$bill. ;$c19 cm.^##$a"A Sports ill
ustrated for kids book."^##$aInstructions for impr
oving soccer skills. Discusses dribbling, heading,
 playmaking, defense, conditioning, mental attitud
e, how to handle problems with coaches, parents, a
nd other players, and the history of soccer.^#0$aS
occer$vJuvenile literature.^#1$aSoccer.^30$aHeads
up guide to super soccer.^ \
```

and includes features and abilities that might not be needed in the Web environment. It is not wrong to use MARC, but we should realize some of the same goals can be achieved in other ways. This realization allows us to ask questions and gives us some intellectual breathing space to consider how we might do the work differently. Might we adopt some standard(s) other than MARC? To begin answering this question, let us look at mark-up systems from worlds outside our own.

NON-LIBRARY MARK-UP LANGUAGES

The purpose of mark-up systems is to define the structural properties of documents (using the term "documents" generically) for later processing. These mark-up systems–which, in this case, should not be considered to be procedural mark-up–should be application-independent. The same data can be redirected and put to multiple uses. This also is true of

MARC, but it involves more work. Prominent examples of mark-up systems are SGML (Standardized General Markup Language), used to control document formatting for publication; HTML (HyperText Markup Language), an application of SGML used to control the display of Web pages; and XML (Extensible Markup Language), a kind of "next generation" version of SGML.

Figure 3 shows an SGML record, with MARC field numbers as a part of it.

Looking at Figure 3 leads one to muse: if the MARC format were being invented now, would it look the same as the MARC format created in the late 1960s? Probably not. Computers are very different now from the way they were then. One of the features of mark-up language is that it uses tags, inserted before and after the data. The tags may or may not be meaningful in human language. They are designed for computers to process, so they need only be meaningful for computers to manipulate according to specified rule sets.

Let us take a look at "Main Entry," defined by MARC tag 100. Why is this personal name in inverted form? Mark-up language prescribes none

FIGURE 3. SGML-MARC Example

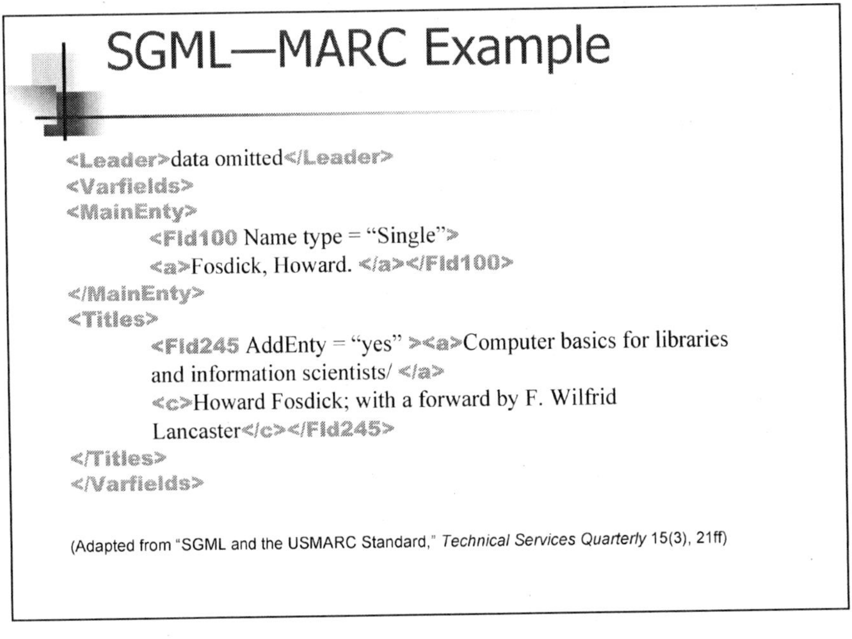

SGML—MARC Example

```
<Leader>data omitted</Leader>
<Varfields>
<MainEnty>
      <Fld100 Name type = "Single">
      <a>Fosdick, Howard. </a></Fld100>
</MainEnty>
<Titles>
      <Fld245 AddEnty = "yes" ><a>Computer basics for libraries
      and information scientists/ </a>
      <c>Howard Fosdick; with a forward by F. Wilfrid
      Lancaster</c></Fld245>
</Titles>
</Varfields>
```

(Adapted from "SGML and the USMARC Standard," *Technical Services Quarterly* 15(3), 21ff)

of that. So, if it is important for useful, accurate resource description to have certain data transcribed and we want them in a certain way and we want certain punctuation, who gets to decide what that is? We do. If we perceive these rules as being essential, we need to speak up if we expect people from non-library worlds to use these rules.

The location of the resource description for a given document can be in several different places. It can be external to the item, for example, bibliographic records in an online catalog, Encoded Archival Description (EAD), or Government Information Location System (GILS). It can be embedded within the resource, for example, Text Encoded Initiative (TEI) or Web page HTML. Or, it can be both internal and external, for example, the combination of Web page headers and a search engine. There are benefits and drawbacks in having resource descriptions in each of these locations. For example, Cataloging-in-Publication on the verso of the title page of a book facilitates getting a book cataloged quickly as it moves through a library's technical services department; but once the book is cataloged and shelved, it has few further uses.

TEI took a giant step forward when it was determined there would be a header portion of every file and one of the parts of that header would be a required text description (similar to a bibliographic citation containing author, title, etc.). It looks like bibliographic information to me. Are these MARC field numbers? No, but, nonetheless, it expresses bibliographic information (see Figure 4).

RESOURCE DESCRIPTION FRAMEWORK

Resource description on the Internet was in a relatively uncontrolled situation, unlike library cataloging using AACR2 and MARC, which is very controlled. Lack of controls has both promise and peril, with the principal peril being that having all those different ways of doing resource description means the benefits of standardization can get lost. What is contained in an individual mark-up standard is determined by an individual community, not by any one group. Then, along comes the World Wide Web Consortium (W3C) saying that the Web needs some framework or structure to constrain mark-up in order to achieve standardization and interoperability of metadata. This brings us to the Resource Description Framework, or RDF.

RDF–a recommendation supported by the World Wide Web Consortium (W3C)–is a group of conventions intended to support interoperability among applications that exchange metadata. RDF is expressed in standard

FIGURE 4. TEI Encoding Initiative

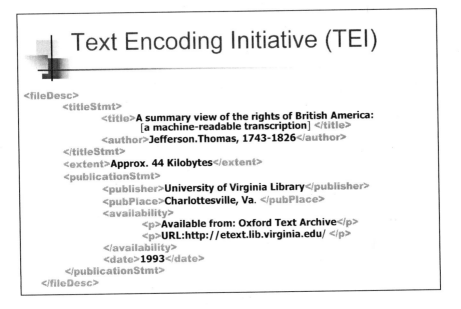

XML in a form that can be processed both by machines and human beings. The content in any one resource description can be defined by a given community or shareholder. Two components underlie RDF: model and syntax.

The model (see Figure 5) is a way of thinking that is helpful to human beings, although computers do not deal with it. It is composed of three parts: oval, arrow, and rectangle. A resource is indicated as an oval, a value is indicated as a rectangle, and a property type is indicated as an arrow going from resource to value. A resource is any item we wish to describe–one can think of it as what you get when you click on a URL. A resource has one or more property types and each type has a value. A property type is like an attribute or a characteristic. Now, this model can be taken from pure theory and put it into practice. Figure 6 uses an English-language name as an example.

Note, especially, that people following RDF are not necessarily following standard library form of entry. Catalogers have a terrific body of rules that explains how to deal most effectively with personal and corporate body names, that is, the rules for authority work. We should make sure we assert ourselves and assist other communities grappling with authority work. A key question here is, "Who gets to establish property types, form of entry, and so forth?" The answer is, "Whoever

FIGURE 5. RDF Model Primitives

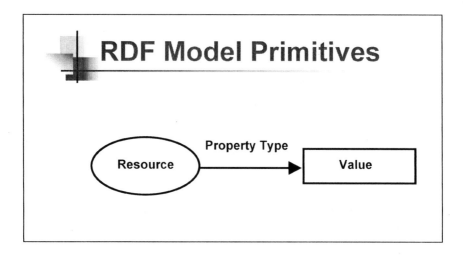

FIGURE 6. RDF Model Example Using Dublin Core Metadata

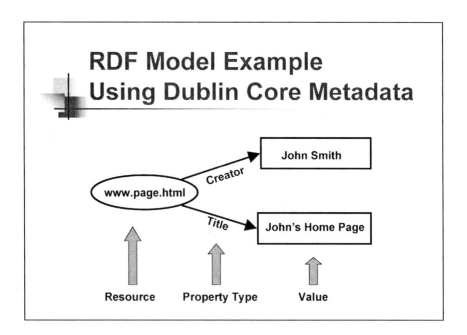

creates the metadata standard." As just stated, if we want metadata to be formulated in accordance with library rules and standards, it is up to us to make it happen.

Now, back to the model. As mentioned above, computers do not deal with these sorts of pictures, so this graphic model needs to be converted into something on which a computer can exercise a set of programmatic instructions. The model needs to be transferred into syntax.

The information in Figure 7 can be processed by a computer if it is given proper instructions. This is XML, which is Unicode-compliant, therefore, it can be embedded into a resource. To do it, we do not have to become RDF/XML programmers. We just need to know enough to understand the situation. I'm pulling the cover back just far enough for us to see and understand its inner workings.

We would never encode this by hand, just as we do not create MARC records by hand.

For the purposes of this discussion, let us ignore the problem of changing URLs and stick to understanding the idea of the RDF standard. Who creates these tag names? It is simultaneously desirable and undesirable that anyone can do so. It is desirable in that no one must uniformly adopt

FIGURE 7. RDF Syntax

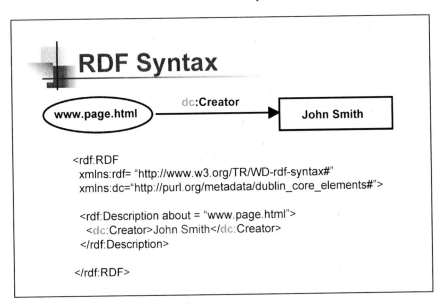

anyone else's tag set and, instead, may develop a tag set appropriate for a given set of resources. On the undesirable side, if that tag set is not uniformly defined, how can anyone else know what each tag means? That brings us to the XML namespace. A namespace is a referencing system, analogous to a See reference. Its purpose is to ensure uniqueness among metadata elements. A namespace declaration looks like the example in Figure 8. It points, via a URL, to somewhere outside the metadata record and explains something about the standard or standards being used (more than one namespace may be given in a record). Thus, it frees the RDF/XML expression from carrying all sorts of information embedded in it (just imagine what a standard catalog record would look like if it had to carry all the AACR2 rules and MARC tagging conventions!) and, also, it assists in getting rid of transcription errors.

The combination of the XML namespace and the URL creates a unique namespace. For example, what if we have a title element in each of two different namespaces? What about the conflict in definition or usage? The answer is to go to each namespace and find out how a given element–in this case, title–is defined in each instance. Now, RDF and the XML namespace can be put together (see Figure 9).

FIGURE 8. Namespace Declaration

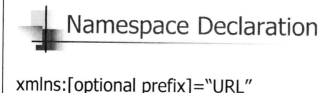

Namespace Declaration

xmlns:[optional prefix]="URL"

xmlns:dc="http://purl.org/metadata/dublin_core_elements#">

xmlns:myPrefix="myURL"

xmlns:yourPrefix="yourURL"

FIGURE 9. Combining RDF and an XML Namespace

```
Putting it All Together

<rdf:RDF xmlns:rdf= "http://www.w3.org/TR/WD-rdf-syntax#"
         xmlns:dc="http://purl.org/metadata/dublin_core_elements#">
         xmlns:bib="http://www.na.org/persons#">
<rdf:Description about = "http://www.page.html">
    <dc:Creator> John Smith </dc:Creator>
<dc:Creator>
    <rdf:Description id="URI:John Smith">
        <bib:Name> John Smith </bib:Name>
        <bib:Email> jsmith@oclc.org </bib:Email>
        <bib:Aff> OCLC </bib:Aff>
        <bib:Aff resource = "http://www.oclc.org"/>
    </rdf:Description>
    </dc:Creator>
    <dc:Title> John's Home Page </dc:Title>
</rdf:Description>
</rdf:RDF>
```

Several different namespaces would be needed for a standard library bibliographic record or for a resource description that uses library rules and tools. (In Figure 9, please note that "bib" is fictitious namespace I made up–do not go to that URL and expect to find anything!) This demonstrates one of RDF and XML namespace's benefits over MARC (as long as the namespace is not "MARC"), which is that a field can be added to a namespace by the namespace owner relatively quickly and readily. We are familiar with the time it takes to get changes into AACR2 (usually measured in years) or into MARC (for example, think of the year-long process to define 856, which was on the Committee on Representation in Machine-Readable Form of Bibliographic Information's (MARBI) "fast track"). In RDF, changes can be accomplished in a few seconds.

Another benefit of RDF is that it enables us to put metadata from multiple sources in same record and do it without ambiguity–to know what each field is and what its source is. Any component typically not contained in a standard bibliographic record, for example, statistics, can be placed unambiguously in a metadata record.

Who is guiding RDF? Not the library world, but rather the World Wide Web Consortium, which, fortunately, does have an ear tuned to the library world. Where can the considerable abilities catalogers have built up over many years be utilized? How about in the areas of form of entry, authority control (for subjects as well as personal and corporate names), classification, etc.–all of the "value-added" things that catalogers do.

METADATA QUESTIONS AND ANSWERS

Who will create metadata? The most likely persons to do this work are librarians, metadata specialists, subject-matter specialists, and resource creators.

When will metadata be created? It can be created when the resource is created, or any time after the resource is created.

How will users create metadata? With file editors or with metadata editing tools; and, in the latter instances, either manually or automatically.

How will metadata be stored? It can be embedded in the resource, or in a searchable database or index, or in both. If it is embedded in the resource, it can be stored as HTML, XML, RDF, or some other format. If it is in a searchable index or database, it will be re-stored as required by specific database applications, such as Oracle, Verity, AltaVista, Excite, OCLC SiteSearch, MS IIS, etc. A sample architecture is to have application programming interfaces between the input form and the database index. Another possibility is to have an application programming interface transform the information in the input form into tagged output, which in turn can be copied and pasted into the resource. Another possibility is to have the process begin with input tagging, which then is processed by a harvester. The application programming interface then transforms the input into database indexes.

CONCLUSION

Here is my time to stand on the soapbox. After air, water, food, and shelter, the next most fundamental need people have is for information. With our long experience of providing organized access to information, we are right near the top of what people need most. But wait, it gets better. Where are libraries found? All around the world. We have the most used container (MARC21), the most widely-used rules (AACR2), classification schemes (Dewey Decimal and Library of Congress classifications), and more. The fundamental question is, "Why is there such a gap between what libraries do and what is happening to information access in non-library land?" Somewhere along the way, a disconnect has occurred. Funding should be pouring in. Where is it? Librarians need to go out and influence information access processes for library users' (and libraries') benefits.

AUTHOR NOTE

A sixteen-year veteran of OCLC Online Computer Library Center, Erik Jul was formerly Executive Director, OCLC Institute, a nonprofit, educational division of OCLC with a global mission to promote the evolution of libraries through advanced education and knowledge exchange. In addition to the OCLC Institute, he has held positions in the OCLC Services Division and the OCLC Office of Research. He has been responsible for market research and analysis, product development and marketing, custom solutions, library consulting, grant development and management, and research.

Beginning in 1991 as a member of the OCLC Office of Research, he managed two U.S. Department of Education funded projects that examined the potential impact of the Internet on traditional library standards and practices. Results of these efforts contributed to the development of MARC field 856, "Electronic Location and Access," and the creation of early cataloging guidelines for Internet resources. He has been a contributor to other emerging standards including the Uniform Resource Locator, the Dublin Core Metadata Element Set, and the Resource Description Framework.

Mr. Jul has served on numerous professional committees and editorial boards including the *Journal of Internet Cataloging, Information Technology and Libraries, LIBRES,* and *Research and Education Networking.*

He holds an MBA from Franklin University, with a focus on knowledge management and organizational leadership, an MA from the Ohio State University, and a BA from Hope College, where he was graduated summa cum laude and inducted into Phi Beta Kappa. He is recipient of the OCLC President's Award, the Meckler Internet Award for Internet Research, and, twice, the Award of Merit from the Society for Technical Communication.

ISSN:
Dumb Number, Smart Solution

Regina Romano Reynolds

SUMMARY. Presents an overview of the ISSN (International Standard Serial Number) in relation to current cataloging codes and evolving metadata standards. Covers the evolution and development of ISSN as a serials identifier; harmonization efforts with AACR2; the functions of identifiers in the electronic age; and the ISSN as a solution to current concerns in areas such as identification of serials and continuing resources, check-in, and obtaining metadata for electronic resources. Issues surrounding multiple manifestations and linking are also discussed. The National Serials Data Program functions as the official ISSN Center in the United States. As such, it works closely with the publishing community in assigning 5,000 to 6,000 ISSN numbers per year to American serials. The ISSN has the potential for identifying and providing access to serials and, in the near future, to many continuing resources as well.

KEYWORDS. ISSN, International Standard Serial Number, National Serials Data Program, United States ISSN Center, international harmonization, AACR2

Regina Romano Reynolds is Head, National Serials Data Program, Library of Congress, 101 Independence Avenue, SE, Washington, DC 20540-4382 (E-mail: rrey@loc.gov).

The article was transcribed by Birdie MacLennan, Coordinator, Serials and Cataloging, University of Vermont.

[Haworth co-indexing entry note]: "ISSN: Dumb Number, Smart Solution." Reynolds, Regina Romano. Co-published simultaneously in *Cataloging & Classification Quarterly* (The Haworth Information Press, an imprint of The Haworth Press, Inc.) Vol. 36, No. 3/4, 2003, pp. 155-171; and: *Electronic Cataloging: AACR2 and Metadata for Serials and Monographs* (ed: Sheila S. Intner, Sally C. Tseng, and Mary Lynette Larsgaard) The Haworth Information Press, an imprint of The Haworth Press, Inc., 2003, pp. 155-171.

http://www.haworthpress.com/store/product.asp?sku=J104
10.1300/J104v36n03_12

BACKGROUND

The ISSN stands for International Standard Serial Number. Compared to numbers with inherent meanings, such as social security numbers in which the prefixes represent the state in which they were issued, the ISSN has no meaning. Thus, one might think of it as a "dumb" number, because no intelligence can be read into it. The ISSN was developed in the early 1970s during an era when science and technology journals were proliferating at exponential rates. A need was perceived for a numerical identifier that would help with record matching, record identification, and finding records in databases that contained large numbers of serials. The ISSN emerged from this environment.

The first seven digits of the ISSN are a random consecutive number. The eighth is a check digit that guards against transcription errors. It is structured to allow for a numerical calculation to be done on the first seven digits, which results in a remainder. The remainder becomes the eighth digit of the ISSN. If the remainder is a "10," the capital letter "X" is used for the eighth digit. Systems such as OCLC perform a calculation on the first seven digits. If the eighth digit is incorrect because of transcription errors in the first seven, OCLC will not accept the number in the 022 $a subfield (for valid ISSNs), but will move it into the 022 $y subfield (for invalid or incorrect ISSNs).

ISSN numbers are currently issued by approximately 72 centers in the ISSN Network, headquartered in Paris. Most centers are located in national libraries around the world. Some are based in scientific or technical centers. The ISSN Network developed a database, called ISSN Online, containing metadata about registered publications. As of August 2001, ISSN Online numbered almost a million records.

In recent years, electronic resources have proliferated rapidly, creating a new environment that provides added impetus for the use of ISSN as an identification tool. Resources are now published in multiple physical formats, each of which needs to be distinguished. At the same time, titles are becoming increasingly difficult to decipher, creating a serious challenge for serials catalogers. When publishers translate their materials from print to online, the use of new technologies, graphics, logos, and/or other innovations of the electronic format sometimes override the need for clear presentation of titles and other identifying information. Cataloging rules do not adequately address the matter of how to identify titles of Websites or online databases. However, if an ISSN is in evidence on the home page, the resource has a clear identifier. In some computer systems, a resource's related metadata, including title, can be searched and retrieved via the ISSN.

Another underlying factor in the evolution of the ISSN is the advent of e-commerce. Publishers realize their resources can be translated into revenues. They are developing methods for packaging or rearranging their information–called "slicing and dicing"–and selling it. One method enabling publishers to collect revenues automatically is an identification system that records how many hits someone makes on an article or how many times a user accesses a resource through a citation. The ISSN and/or the Digital Object Identifier (DOI) are potential identifiers to support such methods.

The ISSN might also play a role in identification schemes for rights management and revenues that may be associated with rights. How does one determine who owns what rights in a publication? Currently, a piecemeal approach is being taken: one person (or publisher or organization) may own the rights to an image in an article, while another owns the rights to the text. Linking resources by ISSN across different systems such as library catalogs, publishers' databases, and citation databases is a promising aspect of possible new uses for the ISSN.

ISSN IN THE TWENTY-FIRST CENTURY

In 1999, the ISSN Network held a Joint ISSN Directors/Governing Board Meeting in Paris at the Bibliothèque Nationale de France to look at the ISSN in the current environment and to plot a course for reinventing the ISSN for the 21st century. During this meeting, the importance of harmonization efforts among the ISSN, AACR2, and International Standard Bibliographic Description for Serials (ISBD(S)) standards was recognized. The ISSN record might serve as a base metadata record on which a library could build for its own catalog. In some countries the ISSN record is, if not the national bibliography record, very close to it. Thus, a one-to-one correspondence among records created under AACR2, ISBD(S), and ISSN rules becomes more important as interest increases in international record sharing as well as finding metadata for resources on the Web that can originate from any country.

The ISSN Network decided to accept and embrace the model of seriality first presented by Hirons and Graham, and later refined by various discussions and work groups.[1] The ISSN Network accepted the definitions for the terms "continuing resources," "integrating resources," and "serials." It accepted the notion that in the near future, ISSNs can be assigned not only to serials in any medium, but also to databases and Websites.

A critical decision had to be made some years ago whether an ISSN should identify a work or a manifestation. Each choice was supported by good reasons. The ISSN would have been a good identifier for pulling together all manifestations of a work, such as the print, online, and CD-ROM versions of the same work. However, the more critical need was felt to be a manifestation level identifier, because the ISSN is used heavily by the publishing community for subscription purposes and by libraries for ordering and claiming. Thus, ISSN evolved into a manifestation level identifier. Separate ISSNs are assigned to each manifestation of a serial and will be assigned in the future to each manifestation of a continuing resource. Multiple manifestations can be pulled together by means of linking ISSNs employing the MARC 776 field. Future development of a work-level identifier appropriate to all manifestations of the same work might also be relevant.

ISSN AND AACR2

Before harmonization, the ISSN record was based on description of the current issue, but afterward, description is based on the earliest issue. The rules for title changes have also been harmonized, aimed at decreasing the number of new records, particularly for insignificant title changes.

Harmonization changes are also evident in the key title. The characteristic space-hyphen-space between the generic term and qualifier was changed to parentheses. Under the new rules, key titles more closely resemble current uniform titles. Development of an International Standard Serial Title (ISST) is under discussion and might be implemented as a replacement for both the key title and the uniform title.

Under the revised rules, construction of the key title consists of the key title plus a parenthetical qualifier. Harmonization of the rules for the title proper under all three standards–an important goal–was largely achieved.

IDENTIFIERS IN THE ELECTRONIC AGE

Identifiers have become popular in the electronic environment. The ISSN Network has been approached by a number of organizations interested in identification. The ISSN is a well-established identifier system and its scope is expanding to include continuing resources, but it is not the sole identifier. Others that merit attention include the Serial Item and Contribution Identifier (SICI), the Digital Object Identifier (DOI), and the Universal Resource Name (URN).

Serial Item and Contribution Identifier (SICI)

The SICI grew out of the print environment. Its scope is serials. The first portion of the SICI is the ISSN and, since the ISSN will cover continuing resources, it seems possible the SICI's scope might expand to include them as well.

Unlike the "dumb" ISSN, the SICI is "smart" because it has inherent meaning in the world of metadata. Its intelligence is that it begins with the ISSN and includes the numerical and chronological designation, a title code, and other details. SICIs consist of three segments: an Item Segment, a Contribution Segment, and a Control Segment. Following are the details, also illustrated in Figure 1:

Item Segment:

- ISSN (first eight digits)
- chronology, given in parentheses
- enumeration, which extends to three levels

Contribution Segment:

- location and title code; the title code is made of the letters of each of the first six words of the title

Control Segment:

- standard version number
- check digit.

The contribution segment extends to the article level, however, when using the SICI to identify the issue level, the contribution segment is not used. The issue level has practical applications in the form of the Serials Industry Systems Advisory Committee (SISAC) barcode, which can be printed on an issue and used for check-in. Some library systems are already using this. It has the potential for increased use if more publishers print the barcode and more vendors develop the capability of making use of it for serials management purposes. Figure 2 illustrates an example of an SICI in which the Contribution Segment identifies an article. It includes the title code "IAA," which stands for the initial letters of the first three words of the title, "Information Age Avatars." This application of "intelligent" code has practical applications for document delivery services.

FIGURE 1. Components of an SICI

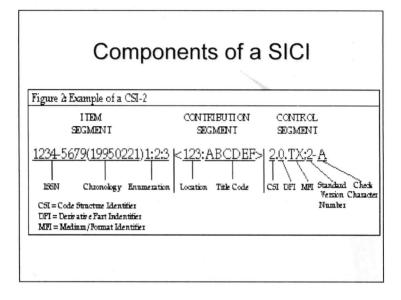

FIGURE 2. SICI for an Article

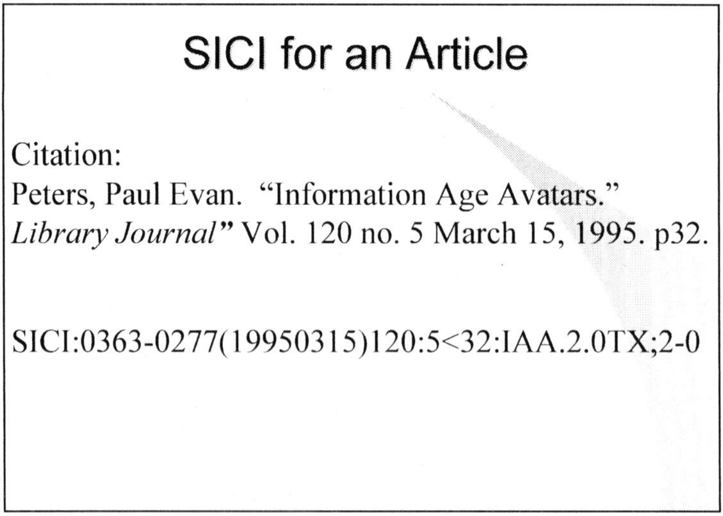

SICI for an Article

Citation:
Peters, Paul Evan. "Information Age Avatars."
Library Journal" Vol. 120 no. 5 March 15, 1995. p32.

SICI:0363-0277(19950315)120:5<32:IAA.2.0TX;2-0

Digital Object Identifier (DOI)

The DOI emerged out of the publishing community. The syntax for the DOI has been accepted as a National Information Standards Organization standard. Many major commercial publishers are using the DOI, notably in cross-reference linking. The goal was to develop the DOI as a tool for publishers to identify individual articles or elements within the articles such as tables, graphics, or related resources, and to collect use statistics and possible revenues on their use. There is a question whether the DOI is intended to serve as a persistent URL (a URN-like identifier) that would eliminate the problem of broken links if the resource was moved to different servers or locations. It has potential as a stable identifier that could work through a resolver service or a translator table to indicate that the object is now at a particular location, not a previous one.

The DOI, at this writing, has not defined rules to clearly distinguish one iteration of the same work from another. If a different publisher assumes rights for a work or an article that was previously published by a different publisher, the new publisher gives it a new DOI. In contrast, in the ISSN system, when a different publisher assumes publication for the same journal and doesn't change the title, the ISSN remains the same. The intention is that the ISSN identifies the resource, not the offering of a particular publisher.

The DOI has fewer prescriptive elements in it than the SICI, which allows more flexibility for publishers. For example, the publisher can choose the suffix portion of the DOI, such as an internal number or an SICI. A central agency does not assign a DOI, the way ISSNs are assigned. Publishers are assigned a DOI prefix followed by a block of numbers administered by the publisher, similar to the way ISBNs work. Thus, the suffix for the publisher can appear in a variety of formats, including the SICI. Figure 3 illustrates this.

Universal Resource Name (URN)

The World Wide Web Consortium is developing the URN as a broad standard for resource identification, much like the URL. Many challenges are inherent in the administration of such a system. The URN is intended to alleviate the problem that arises when resources change location and searchers encounter broken links to previous locations. The current system of linking to the URL is unstable–whenever the resources shift or change servers, the links no longer function. The URN has potential to serve as an identifier in reference-linking systems, which could help libraries reduce catalog and/or web page maintenance.

FIGURE 3. Example of a Digital Object Identifier

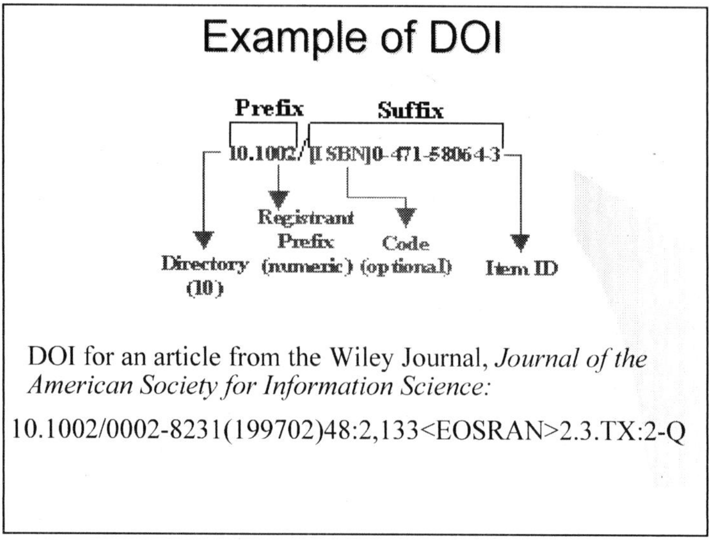
Example of DOI
Prefix
Suffix
10.1002/[ISBN]0-471-58064-3
Registrant
Prefix
(numeric)
Code
(optional)
Directory
(10)
Item ID
DOI for an article from the Wiley Journal, *Journal of the American Society for Information Science:*
10.1002/0002-8231(199702)48:2,133<EOSRAN>2.3.TX:2-Q

If more reference-linking programs were put in place and universally available, it might be best to omit the MARC 856 field from catalog records, but, instead, to let other agencies take care of maintenance by recording all changes in one place. The ISSN has recently become a URN namespace.

SERIALS PROBLEMS AND ISSN SOLUTIONS

Identification is the first problem the ISSN was designed to solve. Naïve users might wonder, "Why do we need a numerical identifier when we have titles? Can't we just use them?" However, many titles are the same or similar, and title identification can be a perplexing task. Title matching doesn't always work. The Library of Congress, for example, has a large backlog of unchecked serial issues that must be searched in the online catalog and the first letter of the titles underlined, so shelvers will know where to place them. Title look-ups are time-consuming, especially when there are as many as 300,000 issues to process. The Library of Congress decided recently to sort the issues by ISSN, because one types in an ISSN and retrieves the title immediately. When the ISSN is printed on serial issues, it speeds ordering, check-in, claiming, subscribing, postal services, and legal deposit.

Barcoding and the ISSN

The SICI, which includes ISSNs, has been translated into barcode. Publishers can wand in their issues with barcode readers for inventory control. Libraries can do the same to check-in serial issues. The author's recent inquiry on a serials discussion list about who was using this capability received several affirmative replies. This is something of a chicken-and-egg issue: If more serials printed the SICI barcode, more systems would make use of it; and if more systems made use of it, more publishers would have reason to print it on their publications. The Library of Congress is investigating the potential of their Voyager system to use SICIs for check-in. Some of the problems include inaccurate SICIs printed on the issues, SICIs printed in ink that bleeds on the issue so the barcode cannot be scanned correctly, and background colors that interfere with scanning. The author's dream vision for solving check-in problems is that 90% of serial issues will have printed barcodes; that ISSN centers will facilitate ensuring the codes are sent to publishers and help given so they understand SICIs importance; and that 90% of the library systems will be able to make use of SICIs to help streamline workflow.

The European equivalent of the Universal Product Code (UPC)–the barcoded number seen on many commercial products in the supermarket–is the European Article Number (EAN). The EAN includes the ISSN, but the UPC does not. EANs (or UPCs) are seen on many newsstand magazines and are scanned by supermarket and bookstore systems. Thus, the ISSN is playing a role in identification for check-in and inventory purposes via SICIs and EANs.

ISSN Online as a Metadata Resource

Another problem is how to obtain sufficient metadata to ensure access to the individual resources included in aggregations. The ISSN Online database has almost a million metadata records for serials that is expanding as ISSNs are assigned to electronic serials and continuing resources. Although ISSN records have fewer fields and less information than CONSER records, they are more complete than publisher-supplied information. ISSN records can be augmented and used as catalog records, or serve as the basis for a brief record for aggregator products in local library databases.

ISSN and Multiple Manifestations

Multiple manifestations of serials have been an ongoing challenge for the ISSN Network. In order to have manifestation-level identifications, a separate ISSN is assigned to each physical format. Some libraries and abstracting and indexing services have found this a problem. The ISSN Network came up with some solutions. In the ISSN database and in CONSER records, the MARC 776 field is used as a linking field to other physical formats. A repeatable subfield, $x, of the 776 field is to be used for ISSNs of other formats. Thus, each record can contain ISSNs for all formats. The ISSN Network is also recommending to publishers that they print the ISSNs of all formats on each one, for example, the publisher of *The Physiologist* displays two ISSNs on the print version, with qualifiers to identify them, shown in Figure 4.

These practices will enable tables of ISSN equivalents to be built, so that the ISSN will be interchangeable across various online systems. Figure 5 is a schematic representation of a structure that can be used as underlying support for ISSNs across online systems. Some online serials management systems, such as SFX (Reference Linking Software Solution, available through Ex Libris), TDNet (Electronic Journals Management System), and Serials Solutions, are making use of such reference-linking systems, treating the ISSN as an equivalent for multiple manifestations. They are interested in delivering content, not manifestations.

The ISSN Network recognizes differences of each manifestation for ordering, pricing, and claiming mechanisms. Additionally, different

FIGURE 4. Journal with Multiple ISSNs

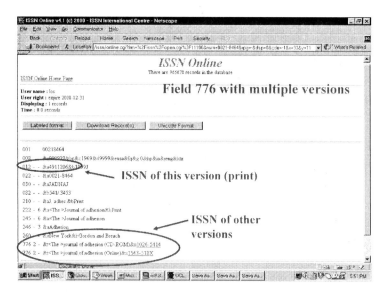

FIGURE 5. Sample Table of Equivalents

Title	Print	Online	CD-ROM
Callaloo	0161-2492	1080-6512	
American journal of mathematics	0002-9327	1080-6377	
Point line poly	1099-2324	1099-2774	
The Journal of biological chemistry	0021-9258	1083-351X	1067-8816
Physical review letters	0031-9007	1079-7114	1092-0145
Laboratory robotics and automation	0895-7533	1098-2728	

manifestations have different rights associated with them. By assigning different ISSNs to each manifestation and pulling them together via tables of equivalents for reference linking systems, both the similarities and the differences can be recognized and represented.

Future development on a work-level identifier appropriate to all manifestations of the same work might also be relevant for bringing different manifestations of serials and continuing resources together in the online environment. The International Standard Textual Code (ISTC)–an evolving work-level identifier that has grown out of special needs of music identification–offers a possible model. The ISTC is for textual works and may have applicability to continuing resources. An International Standards Organization (ISO) group is working on it.

ISSN AND ELECTRONIC LINKING

Electronic linking is a power tool. As mentioned, linking by ISSN is more reliable than linking by title. The ISSN can be a key link between data from the local catalog or Web page and metadata in the online environment.

The ISSN recently became a URN (Universal Resource Number) namespace. The National Serials Data Program has been involved in a pilot project permitting the ISSN to link both to the resource and the metadata about the resource with a downloadable plug-in available to anyone via the ISSN Website. This plug-in application, illustrated in Figure 6, allows users to type the ISSN into a browser and retrieve both the record and the resource at the same time.

The ISSN can also function as a catalog link allowing a connection from the catalog record for a serial to outlying electronic resources. Some possible applications include:

- A "hook to holdings" that connects a citation in an abstracting and indexing service database to a bibliographic record and its holdings data in a library catalog. Figure 7 shows an article citation, a journal title, and related library holdings data from a catalog all on one screen display, made possible by ISSN linking between the systems. The display enables the end-user to know immediately if the library has the issue containing the particular article retrieved from a citation index.
- The ISSN, through the MARC 780 and 785 fields and other horizontal links can enable displays of earlier/later/related linked titles in a diagram approach, similar to a genealogical chart or family tree. (See Figure 8.)
- Links can display acquisitions information between systems. For example, *Ulrichs Periodical Directory* has information that overlaps with catalog information and also offers other acquisitions and subscription information not usually provided in the catalog. ISSNs could provide a useful match in linking to this external metadata.
- Links to external sources which provide information about where specific titles are indexed, where they are available, and what dates are covered could be made in the catalog record via the ISSN. For example, the School of Medicine at Yale University's Jointly Administered Knowledge Environment system, known as "jake," is a reference source for finding, managing, and linking online journals and journal articles. It has been emulated by some commercial linking services.

ISSN: Catalog to Aggregator Link

How libraries inform their users of the titles purchased in large aggregations is a challenge and the subject of much discussion. One of the problems is the availiability of copy through a variety of aggregated sources. For example, a resource may be available through EBSCOHost, IDEAL, ScienceDirect, and other sources. The questions are: to which sources has the library subscribed and how can users best be connected to them? Some libraries have developed local solutions and there are also some commercial solutions. Some companies, notably Serials Solutions, Ex-Libris's SFX, and TDNet, work with libraries to develop lists of the resources to which the library subscribes and, then, create links to them.

FIGURE 6. ISSN as URN Namespace Pilot Project Example 1–LC Staff Home Page

FIGURE 7. ISSN as URN Namespace Pilot Project Example 2

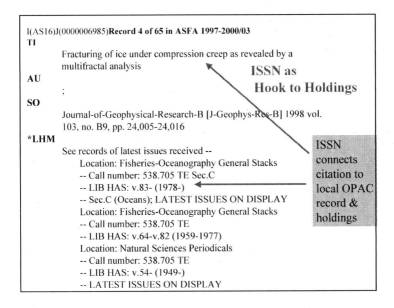

FIGURE 8. Genealogical Tree of a Family of Serials Linked by Their ISSNs

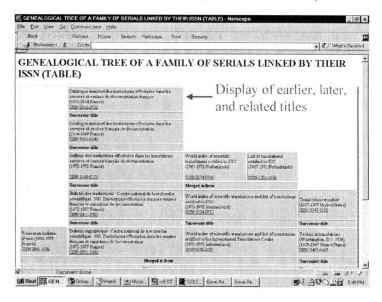

ISSN REGISTRATION–
LINKING PUBLISHERS AND LIBRARIES

ISSN centers throughout the world collaborate regularly with the publishing community. Publishers send metadata about their publications to ISSN centers on forms provided by the centers. ISSN centers can, in turn, format the metadata so it can be sent back to the publishers and embedded in the resources, thus making this structured metadata more widely available.

The National Serials Data Program has developed an online registration form that solicits the same kind of metadata from publishers that will be used in the MARC 21 record. (See Figure 9.) Behind the Web application form is a program that converts the data supplied by the publisher into MARC 21 tags and outputs a draft MARC 21 record. For example, the data the publisher puts in the "publisher" box on the form is converted to a MARC 260 field. A cataloger then takes this metadata and edits the draft record to conform to MARC 21 and AACR2 standards. At this point, the edited MARC record can be converted to HTML via conversion software, such as OCLC's Cooperative Online Resource Catalog (CORC). The HTML record can then be sent back to

FIGURE 9. NSDP Web Application Form

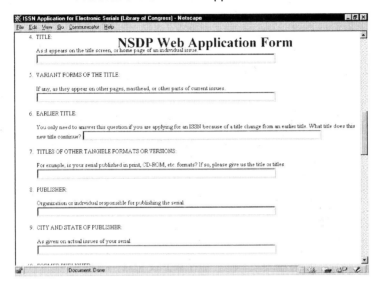

the publisher along with the ISSN and be embedded in the resource. When mounted on the Web, the data are available to search engines, which can take advantage of structured data in record headers.

One of the remarkable things about this process is the link that ISSN centers provide between publishers and libraries. Publishers come to the National Serials Data Program at the prepublication stage seeking an ISSN. The Program assigns the ISSN and, at the same time, raises publisher awareness about the ways libraries manage subscriptions and provide access to serial publications using the ISSN and other forms of metadata to link end users with the information they seek. The Program is able to encourage use of the SICI barcode and other standards because publishers recognize the importance of the ISSN as an identifier. The author hopes the Program will succeed in raising awareness about the importance of developing metadata standards and implementing them.

Many potential benefits for libraries can result. Baseline catalog records that can be derived from publishers' metadata might be one result. A reverse conversion program might be used to take HTML and create a basic MARC 21 record. Then, a local library could enhance the basic record. CORC pathfinders could be created from these records and improved search engine results might occur. A subset of *Library of Congress Subject Headings* might also be developed, or a mapping scheme to them from the subject headings used by publishers (such as the BASIC subject heading list), so publishers can include subject headings in the metadata they give to the Program. ISSN records do not currently include subject headings, though they do provide three digits of a Dewey class number. These are but a few of the ways in which ISSNs can be used to achieve faster, better access for the people who need information.

CONCLUSION

The ISSN may be a dumb number, but it has provided the key to smart solutions for a variety of problems, described and illustrated above. It offers still greater potential for future solutions to the new problems being encountered in today's online environment.

AUTHOR NOTE

Regina Romano Reynolds has been head of the National Serials Data Program, the U.S. ISSN center, since 1992. She has worked at the Library of Congress since 1976 and has spent much of her professional career explaining and promoting serials standards, particularly the ISSN, to librarians, publishers, and the information community. At LC, Ms. Reynolds is a member of the Bibliographic Enrichment Advisory Team (BEAT), a research and development team charged with the "development and implementation of initiatives to improve the tools, content, and access to bibliographic information" and was instrumental in the development of BEAT's BEOnline Project for cataloging Internet resources. She also chaired the CONSER Task Force on Electronic Resources and is one of the original co-authors of *CONSER Cataloging Manual* Module 31 for cataloging online resources. Ms. Reynolds is active in ALA, where she is LC's liaison to the Committee to Study Serials Cataloging, consultant to the Committee to Study Serials Standards, and was one of the original members of the ALCTS Networked Resources and Metadata Committee. She is also a frequent presenter at ALA Institutes and at North American Serials Institute (NASIG) meetings on electronic resources and metadata topics. She is on the Editorial Board of *Serials Review* and has authored numerous articles on ISSN, cataloging, and serials standards for various professional publications. Such articles include "Harmonizing Bibliographic Control of Serials in the Digital Age," "Back to the Future of AACR: Retooling Former Cataloging Practices to Solve Problems Old and New" and "Seriality and the Web." Ms. Reynolds was a presenter at the Library of Congress's Bicentennial Conference on Bibliographic Control for the New Millennium where she spoke on "Partnerships to Mine Unexploited Sources of Metadata." She has been actively involved in the revision of AACR2 to accommodate seriality and electronic resources, and in the international harmonization of serial cataloging rules and standards. Ms. Reynolds was the 1999 recipient of the Bowker/Ulrich's Serials Librarian Award. She has an MLS (Beta Phi Mu) from the University of Michigan and undergraduate degrees in English and French from the University of Dayton.

REFERENCE

1. Jean Hirons and Crystal Graham, "Issues Related to Seriality," In *The Principles and Future of AACR: Proceedings of the International Conference on the Principles and Future Development of AACR, Toronto, Ontario, Canada, October 23-25, 1997,* Jean Weihs, ed. (Ottawa: Canadian Library Association . . . , 1998); additional papers are available at the CONSER website, http://lcweb.loc.gov/acq/conser/seriality.html.

Index

Page numbers followed by f indicate figures.